SAM 48
(MY WAY)

By
Dave Costello

MAPLE
PUBLISHERS

SAM 48 (MY WAY)

Author: Dave Costello

Copyright © 2025 Dave Costello

The right of Dave Costello to be identified as author of this work has been asserted by the author in accordance with section 77 and 78 of the Copyright, Designs and Patents Act 1988.

ISBN 978-1-83538-502-9 (Paperback)
　　　978-1-83538-503-6 (E-Book)

Book Cover Design and Layout by:
　　　White Magic Studios
　　　www.whitemagicstudios.co.uk

Published by:
　　　Maple Publishers
　　　Fairbourne Drive, Atterbury,
　　　Milton Keynes,
　　　MK10 9RG, UK
　　　www.maplepublishers.com

A CIP catalogue record for this title is available from the British Library.

All rights reserved. No part of this book may be reproduced or translated by any form or by any means, electronic or mechanical, including photocopying, recording or by any information storage and retrieval system without written permission from the author.

The views expressed in this work are solely those of the author and do not necessarily reflect the views of the publisher, and the publisher hereby disclaims any responsibility for them.

CONTENTS

Dedication 10
My School Days 11
My Future Life 13
Chapter 1 – The Introduction 14
    1-1 Panda 15
    1-2 The Potato 16
    1-3 The Snowball 16
    1-4 The Time Clock 18
    1-5 War 19
    1-6 The Wash Bay 20
    1-7 The Body 21
    1-8 Roller Bearings 22
    1-9 The Crane 23
    1-10 The Broom 24
    1-11 Dino's Revenge 25
    1-12 Friday Nights 26
Chapter 2 – The Pits Construction 28
    2-1 This is just a hole in the floor, or is it? 28
    2-2 Pit Boards 28
    2-3 Enter Jim 29
    2-4 Underground Football 29
    2-5 Oily's Baccy 30
    2-6 Mini Skirts 31
    2-7 Fire Down Below 32
    2-8 The Bell 33

Chapter 3 – Accidents 35

3-1 First Free Service of a New Ford Zephyr 35

3-2 The Old Hill 36

3-3 The Horse 37

3-4 Aluminium Housing 37

3-5 Forklift 38

3-6 The Forklift's Second Appearance 39

3-7 The Model T 40

3-8 The Rewire 41

3-9 Moving On 42

3-10 A Loving Couple 42

3-11 The Villains 43

3-12 Things That Fell Off 44

3-13 Harry 45

Chapter 4 – Tests and Bombs 47

4-1 Headlamps, Tests and More 47

4-2 Finals Day 47

4-3 The Test 49

4-4 The Banquet 50

4-5 The On-Site Presentation 50

4-6 Tail Lights 52

4-7 Bolt Bombs 52

4-8 Respray 53

4-9 V8 Pilot 54

4-10 Brake Blocks 55

4-11 Mr Ron 55

Chapter 5 – Innocent Victims 56

5-1 Whale Oil 56

5-2 Hiram 57

    5-3 Hiram Again 58

    5-4 Tom The Fossil 58

    5-5 Lost One 60

Chapter 6 – Tricks and Gifts 61

    6-1 The Sandwich 61

    6-2 The Tannoy 62

    6-3 Our Chief Accountant 62

    6-4 Redex 63

    6-5 Radiator Blind 64

    6-6 The Box 65

    6-7 Swaeooo 66

    6-8 Our Pet RIP 67

    6-9 The Challenge 68

    6-10 The Second Challenge 69

    6-11 Eleven on the Calculator 69

    6-12 The Rose Bowl 70

    6-13 The Rag Bag 71

    6-14 Grandad 71

    6-15 Our Rep Fran 73

    6-16 Our Rep Bobby 74

    6-17 The Gift 75

    6-18 The Non-spider 76

    6-19 The Non-spider – Two 77

    6-20 Wreckers 77

    6-21 The Fire Alarm 79

    6-22 The Hanging 79

    6-23 The VW Trade Launch 81

    6-24 Pilot Boats 82

Chapter 7 – Vicar, Vermin, International 84

7-1 The Vicar 84

7-2 Dustcart 86

7-3 Dollies 87

7-4 The Nose 88

7-5 Hydraulic Ram 90

7-6 The Pajero 90

7-7 Mr Dance 92

7-8 The Segwin 94

7-9 Delphi Call Up 96

7-10 Invite to Germany, Luckily 97

7-11 Signage 99

7-12 Number Plates 99

7-13 Second-Hand Cars 100

7-14 My XR3 101

7-15 Ford's Indian 101

7-16 Help Yourself 102

7-17 The Golden Arrow 103

7-18 Pigeon 104

7-19 The Seagulls 105

7-20 Our Christmas Bonus 106

7-21 Our Christmas Draw 107

7-22 Air Tubes 107

7-23 The Wasp Nest 108

7-24 Blackberries 109

7-25 The Italian Truck 110

Chapter 8 – Social Club 111

8-1 Car Rally 111

    8-2 Car Rally 2 112

    8-3 Football Team 113

    8-4 In Nick.. 113

    8-5 Married Versus Singles 114

    8-6 Town Team Versus The New Depots 115

    8-7 5-A-Side Challenge... 116

    8-8 The Football Final 116

    8-9 Indoor Cricket... 117

    8-10 The Cricket Team.. 118

    8-11 Cricket at High Halstow 118

    8-12 Ghost Trip 119

    8-13 The Ghost Trip Continues 120

    8-14 Quiz Nights.. 120

    8-15 London Shows 121

    8-16 Gliding.. 122

    8-17 Ten-Pin Bowling.. 123

    8-18 Coach Trip to See the Christmas Lights 123

    8-19 Dog Racing... 124

    8-20 Trip to Poole in Dorset.. 125

    8-21 First International Trip... 126

    8-22 Trip To Paris 127

    8-23 24 Hours of Le Mans 128

    8-24 The Christmas Social 129

Chapter 9 – Technical College **132**

    9-1 Further Learning 132

    9-2 The Bounce 132

    9-3 General Studies 133

    9-4 Tyre Change 134

9-5 Lead Wings 135

9-6 The Forge 136

9-7 The Shared Canteen 136

9-8 Smoking 137

9-9 The Megger 137

9-10 The Automatic Gearbox 138

9-11 Lunchtime 138

9-12 Lunchtime Meals 140

Chapter 10 – Repairs of a Different Kind 141

10-1 My Manager 141

10-2 The Fuse 141

10-3 Watch and Clock Repairs 143

10-4 Alternators 144

10-5 Snuff 145

10-6 Turbochargers 145

10-7 The Polished Element 146

10-8 Wine 148

10-9 Oil Heaters 148

10-10 Chads 150

10-11 Threepenny Bit Tyres 151

10-12 The Navy Lark 152

10-13 The Navy Lark Continues 153

10-14 It Goes On 155

Chapter 11 – Toilets and Cubicles 156

11-1 The Toilet Block 156

11-2 Georgiou 156

11-3 The Cubicles 157

11-4 The Fountain 157

11-5 The Stretcher 158

11-6 First-Aid Box 159

11-7 The Deflector 159

Chapter 12 – The New Building 160

12-1 The Search 160

12-2 Next Door 160

12-3 My Former Boss 161

12-4 The C5 and the Jaguar 162

12-5 Jock 164

Chapter 13 – Our Claim to Fame 166

13-1 The Bucking Bronco 166

13-2 Smoking Area 168

Chapter 14 – Tools and Cash 170

14-1 New Specialist Tools 170

14-2 Old Unit Box 172

14-3 The Cash Box 173

Chapter 15 – The New PC System 175

15-1 All Hail the System 175

15-2 The Impossible Task 175

15-3 Sales Dip 176

15-4 Time to Go 178

Chapter 16 – Some of the Staff and Supporting Cast 179

Dedication

I would like to thank many people for making this book happen.

My school teachers and classmates for understanding me.

My friends and my experiences with them during my youth club years. Also, a special mention of the band of brothers who guided me through my apprenticeship and on to a fairly successful career in the motor trade. The teaching staff at the night school, whose good input enabled me to gain The Fellow of the Institute of the Motor Industry (FIMI) status when I was just 24 years old.

But again, back to the band of brothers without whose input it would have made a very dull life.

I would like to thank the Kent Police for never capturing me, except when I rode my pushbike on the footpath.

My family has been fully behind me throughout my life sentence to the motor trade. One absent friend was the director who got me underway. A certain Mr D.

Time moved on, and there came a change of direction—starting my own company with my landlord, J.B., showing me a different way of life.

This book was conceived on a beach in Kos, with many headings just scribbled down for later use. Thanks to all of our Greek friends.

For pushing me towards having it published, I have to thank Wilf, my neighbour, and Butch, a fellow engineer, who has also put pen to paper.

My School Days

I received my education at a Secondary Modern School, a good school with a good set of teachers.

At the time of the eleven-plus, there was a decision to be made. Option one was to try hard and go to the Boys' Technical School. This was across town, approximately five miles away, so with no family car, buses and legs were the only option.

Option two was Maidstone Grammar School. This was of no interest to me. You had to be clever, have a reasonably wealthy family and be prepared to do heaps of homework. It was not an issue as I couldn't qualify for it on any of the criteria. Plus, the Grammer Grubs were always a target for a good hiding.

My mum was a little disappointed that I did not pass the eleven-plus, as she called it. Deep inside, I was happy as all my chums also blew out on a better level of education. So, Secondary School it was.

Our class was 30-plus strong, all boys, so the classes were further subdivided into quarters or houses as they were known. The best house was the South. Red was its assigned colour. I think eight from our class, plus eight from each of the other two classes in our year were assigned to the South during registration when we arrived.

Fortunately, I was allocated to the South. Lucky break!

The South had a monopoly on sports. Ten of the twelve needed for the football team came from here. The same bunch also played cricket and basketball in addition to athletics, so it was fair to say we had sports tied up.

We all did learn a little outside the sports area. Maths, OK. English, History and Geography, could have done better. Religious Instruction, Music and Art left me wanting.

Apart from a small fire caused by phosphorus that was accidentally dropped into a dustbin containing sawdust and wastepaper, Science was a good subject.

The only other subject that I recall is our gardening lesson, during which most of the spades and shovels were buried under the soil.

Only two of each were returned to the shed where the gardening equipment was stored. I never found out if any of those tools ever grew, let alone flower.

I did master the triangle in Music, but everything else went completely over my head.

My Future Life

During our last year at school, our career advisor helped most of us get placements. I wanted to be an Electrician as my father worked for The Electricity Board. I did not want to be a vet, join the armed forces, work outdoors in the cold and wet as a farmer or become a construction engineer.

The electrician roles never quite worked out. However, there were openings at a couple of the local garages as they needed to stock up with cheap labour. There were seven vacancies to apply for, five for apprentice motor fitters and two for parts trainees.

Interviews were arranged.

It is quite an ordeal for a fifteen-year-old to be grilled by a wealthy, middle-aged, upper-class gentleman. During my interview, he dropped the piece of information into the conversation that he had been racing at Brands Hatch over the weekend.

Did I see any racing on TV?

Without much hesitation, I said, "Yes, but the Zephyr you were driving, I believe you ended up with it upside down."

The man chuckled. I thought I had blown it. Two days later, surprisingly, I received a letter of offer in the post for an apprenticeship, which I gratefully accepted.

Both my parents were as excited as I was. My future had an outline.

Chapter 1

The Introduction

We were asked to be at the company's reception at 8 a.m. on Monday morning. All five prospective vehicle engineers were lined up and given a badge with our name on each. The thought flashed through my mind that if we were shot, the name badges would identify our bodies.

When I first joined the company, our workshop had an excellent collection of characters, twenty technicians. They varied from sparkies and grease monkeys to locksmiths, vehicle preparers, road testers, fitters and others.

There was a workshop foreman and his deputy, the chargehand. The five new apprentices were to join this band of brothers.

The first day was challenging. We, the five intakes straight from school, were introduced to the workforce. To my astonishment, fourteen of the technicians were Daves with two more Daves in the five newbies.

I thought the name situation could be a problem, but it was soon resolved. The phone rang, and there was an urgent call for Dave Willis. So, the foreman Andy announced over the Tannoy that there was a phone call for Dave.

The general silence was immediately broken with all fourteen Daves cheering and hooting in unison before Andy could get to announce the surname.

I knew then that this was going to be a good crack of a place to work.

All the Daves had nicknames: Weasel – Woosack – Bumble – Barney – Blackie – Whitey – Holly – Joe – Grommet – Willy – Beaky and many more. My handle became Sam, and to this day, many still call me that, both within the company and outside, as many of our regular customers used this and still do. Some think that is my real birth name.

1-1 Panda

Our friend Panda was the grease monkey. He had no ambition, no sense of humour, in fact, he did not have much going for him at all.

Six feet four inches when roused to his full height, he would flap his arms, looking like a king penguin. He was always a good target for abuse, not bullying, but for soft humour. His grease gun always leaked more grease than all the others added together.

When I asked why this was so, Bumble said the O-ring seal had been removed "for safe keeping" without Panda's knowledge. This O-ring was essential to keep the grease inside the grease gun. The handle of his grease gun was, therefore, always slippery, and the trigger for pumping grease to the desired spot made this operation random. Grease was everywhere, some even found its way into the intended target, the grease nipple.

One day, Panda was lowering the lift while standing beneath it. There was no notice or warning sign to say this was not a good idea. The lever to lower the lift is out of reach for average-size humans, but Panda was exceptionally tall. The descending lift and Panda's head had a coming together of sorts.

Fortunately, the lift was not damaged, but Panda was out cold, lying flat on the floor. After a few seconds, there was movement, which was fortunate because nobody volunteered to give him mouth-to-mouth.

No lasting damage to either the lift or to an embarrassed Panda.

A lesson in where not to stand while the lift descends.

Our friendly signwriter did make a belated contribution with an advisory notice: Beware—Low-Flying Lift

This sign stayed in place for many years. Panda had, fortunately, learnt his lesson.

1-2 The Potato

I settled in reasonably quickly, the chaps were all good-natured and very helpful. There was no excuse for missing a variety of options to brighten the day and integrate some sport into it.

One day, a small commercial vehicle entered the workshop for a minor repair. It was also to be our fix for fun.

It was the local fruit and vegetable delivery truck fully laden with wares for sale. Soon after its arrival, one of the bags of baking potatoes somehow miraculously split. What could be more convenient than such an offering being presented to us! With the new arrival of "potato footballs" from the truck, customers' cars were pushed to one side.

It was game on.

Daves versus the rest. It was the Daves who kicked off. Being a little better than average, I got stuck in.

It was a chip (excuse the pun) that I lifted clear off the goalie (Goose) that managed to take out a window directly behind the stranded Goose.

There was a sudden silence. People froze. There was the sound of glass falling to the ground.

The noise went on forever as the next four panes of glass fell—the whole vertical row of glass was now on the ground.

The glass had been fitted as a greenhouse glass, where the first pane holds the second and so on, with small clips.

Jacko, the saviour, was summoned. He was the odd-job man and the maintenance engineer. Very quickly, all was back to normal—a good sweep-up and cars pushed back to their repair stations.

As usual, and to my relief, no one saw anything. The bag of potatoes was repacked, just a couple of potatoes lighter.

1-3 The Snowball

By now, I had been employed for some months. Winter was full of heavy snowfall. Vehicles, when brought to the workshop, had an excellent covering of snow on arrival. The norm was to brush the snow off to avoid a soggy workshop.

If that action was missed, the Daves had ammunition to shower the rest with round, snowy objects. Snowballs rained relentlessly, and some people took refuge in the electricians' lockup. The lockup was a secure area where all the radios and other delicate electrical items were stored.

The contents of the lockup were new-fangled things like radios and early control units before ECUs became commonplace. Batteries were charged using a heavy charger that buzzed constantly. This secure area was a large room with welded mesh panels above the door, right up to the ceiling, for security.

From my vantage point, I saw Daisy May. He was a legitimate target. He thought he was out of range.

I thought I could aim 44 feet, about two cricket pitches in length and just past the door. I had Daisy May in my sight.

Rolled one up, aimed and launched.

Just a little too high for Daisy, but I did hit the welded mesh security covering above the electricians' lockup door. The snowball disintegrated on impact. The snow eventually went back to its natural state, water.

But first, this slush—now melting snow—was entering just about every box with a radio inside. The conclusion was that snow stopped our play, and we were in trouble.

Miraculously, a large hole appeared in the ceiling above the lockup. This sheet of corrugated asbestos, which must have caused the issue of the snow ingress, had moved.

Our thanks went to Jacko who deliberately manufactured this hole by sliding the asbestos roof panel forward. He did this while it was still full-on snowing, preventing any suspicion of foul play. As the disaster unfolded, this hole in the roof was undoubtedly where the problem had originated.

The very next morning, Jacko urgently fixed the same hole he had created, sliding the panel back into position.

He even fitted back the same four nails he had removed earlier. After the inquiry was complete, I rewarded Jacko with a Brown and Mild. In the local ale house, a big cheer went up from all those present as disaster had been averted.

1-4 The Time Clock

As was the culture in the 1960s, a clocking-in system was on hand to detect staff attendance.

The main clock, resembling an antique grandfather clock, was wall-mounted in the service bay. The clock was six feet high and glass-fronted with a proper wooden frame. The clock face had Roman numbers, and it had a pendulum that swung methodically below the face. It was wired to the stations across the company for each department to have identical timekeeping.

Before the regulation time began, it was customary for Ron to teach me and Grovsie his wrestling skills. Ron and Geoff, our mentors, usually tried to give us a hard time.

We had improved our skills through Ron's tuition as he was a blackbelt Judo instructor. We jumped Geoff, and with a two-to-one advantage, we overcame his resistance. He fell backwards.

Using Geoff's body weight, with me and Grovsie assisting, we charged Ron. The force of the three bodies unbalanced Ron. He staggered backwards with a resounding chain of events. Ron's butt took out the clock in one go. The clock glass was on the floor. A hasty truce was called.

The phone rang.

All four of us were called to the General Manager's office, which looked down on the whole workshop.

An explanation was necessary. Geoff had tripped, and Ron attempted to save him from falling. Grovsie and I tried in vain to stop Geoff's fall.

The GM said he saw all that had happened.

He suggested that we apprentices offer a shilling, a "voluntary" contribution, to repair the clock's glass.

Both Ron and Geoff agreed that a donation of half-a-crown each should compensate for the unfortunate "accident".

Ron was also told by the GM to sharpen up and not let the youngsters outdo his Judo skills.

We lived on for another day.

1-5 War

The commercial workshop was on the upper level, which consisted of a strange yet hostile bunch of renegade engineers.

They were distinct by their workwear. Green overalls. They only repaired the trucks, or lorries as they were known. These engineers were, generally, a lot bigger than us delicate car technicians.

The spare parts area for all the technicians was a shared room, probably nine feet square. It was located off the car workshop, which made it necessary for the commercial boys to venture through hostile territory. The parts area served both car and commercial spares.

Our engine wash bay was next door to the parts serving area and had a long hose used primarily for washing engines.

If a single commercial employee dared to enter our space, he was either greased, oiled or washed down. Other options were also available. Most of the time, the commies, as they were known, came down in pairs. For a more serious rumble, a whole bunch would turn up. Nobody was ever injured, but lots of grease, water and oil were used. Sleeves of the overalls, pockets and even belts were good trophies for our display cabinet.

The most serious injury was Big Jack No Toes having his belt removed from his sixty-inch waist trousers. The only thing now holding Jack's trousers up were his overalls.

The belt buckle was hung high in our trophy cabinet as it took seven car apprentices to win that prize. The remainder of the belt was posted back to Jack in the internal post to remind him of his torment.

1-6 The Wash Bay

When cleaning the workshop, the engine wash bay was of particular interest to me. Each morning, before the real work got underway, it was customary to use the broom and sweep it up.

The garage was, at best, mature, but there's no excuse for leaving rubbish on the floor. Within the first quarter of an hour, it was as clean as it could be.

The engine wash bay was different. It had oil, grime, dirt, paint and more. It was good to wash anything that needed washing in this space.

At the back was a trough with paraffin in it. It had a lid, but the lid was almost never used.

On the floor was a steel mesh covering a collector bucket. The mesh was about two yards square. It was heavy, and it took two people to lift it up.

The water, which was constantly in use, diluted any waste, and, I guess, it went into the sewer. The collector bucket was removed and cleaned only about once each week. I liked playing with water. High pressure made it more fun.

The wash area was sort of my pet project, and I took pride in cleaning this area. After a few months of this obsession of mine, it started looking a lot better than when I had started. If so much as a cigarette end was thrown on the floor, I could chase it with the hose. It would have been easier picking it up, but the fun in washing it to its final resting place made my day.

Our chargehand, Bob, was aware of the time spent cleaning this area daily. We had the steel cover off, and it was leaning against the wall. The collector bucket was half full and needed emptying.

The ever-diligent Bob came over to show us how it should be done.

Bearing in mind that I had this place good and tidy and the best it had looked in years, I was annoyed and acted on it. A quick turning up of the pressure valve to flat-out force, and Bob, hose in hand, was out of control. Water was splashing everywhere.

Bob was not quite in control as his left leg went where the collector bucket was. It was in the moiré, just about to his knee. One of his work boots was now soaked. We helped him recover, and we turned off the water. It was funny, and we tried not to laugh but failed. His left leg was like a chubby dipstick.

After ensuring he was not injured, Bob just walked away. The trail of oil went from the wash to the office.

He disappeared for a couple of hours and returned with clean clothes and dry shoes. Never again did he interfere with my cleaning technique for this area.

1-7 The Body

Ron, after serving many years as a good engineer, was promoted to chargehand. We needed to celebrate in style.

A pair of overalls was taken from the locker area, along with all the old boxes. Newspapers and polystyrene were also gathered.

Tom's old, size-twelve boots were seconded and tied to the overall's legs. The overalls were filled with cardboard and other collected waste material. We were now ready.

Lunchtime was declared by the 1 p.m. bell. Ron disappeared into the canteen to swallow his sandwiches.

An innocent Cortina was jacked up, and the headless overalls were placed under the vehicle's wheel. The jack was then removed.

The legs were visible with a pair of boots sticking out. Who was it? Was he dead? Ron returned to the scene and, with his immense strength, lifted the wing and pulled the "body" forward.

He potentially saved the life of the overalls.

Twenty or so heads were secretly watching. Once it was established that there was no loss of life, all the viewers disappeared in all directions for fear of repercussions.

Ron's bad language went on for some time before we dared return to carry out our appointed tasks.

1-8 Roller Bearings

It's a subject to be avoided, dangerous and against all health and safety guidelines (even at the time).

A roller bearing is an essential item in every vehicle. It's necessary to replace it when it's worn out. Once worn out, it has no value except as scrap metal. But to an apprentice, it's a weapon.

Bearings come in all sizes, the larger the bearing, the more the weight it carries. The real Mamma Jo-Jo bearing was the rear-half shaft bearing. It's three inches in diameter and just about as heavy as it could get.

Once it's cleaned and oiled, the bearing can generally be freely rotated by hand. The expertise was in only using bearings that had no potential to seize up, as injury would be an issue, for sure.

Imagine the extra rotation that could be achieved with the aid of a compressed airline hose. Holding the centre track of the bearing, the outer track spins at a very high speed due to its air assistance.

First the noise. It resembles a jet engine increasing its tempo on take-off. Holding the bearing now is a challenge. Its inertia is trying to get the inner track to catch up with the outer track's speed.

Our garage is probably fifty feet wide, two car lengths with a centre driveway of 10 feet and steel benches against both walls.

The bearing is hard to handle when it spins rapidly. It has a gyroscopic effect. Aim is critical.

So, once the bearing is released in full flow, it quickly accelerates across the floor. The gyroscopic force is considerable, with sparks flying, as the steel tries to grip the concrete. The bearing's outer track is picking up speed, and with each yard it covers, it generates even more speed.

By the time the bearing has reached its target, it's probably approaching 50 mph. The aim was generally Tom's boots. Tom would have been wearing them at the time, although as the bearing is still accelerating, if it misses the boot, it would climb the wall for a few feet.

The wall by Tom's bench had many lumps of plaster missing to add to his ever-growing collection of used bearings.

1-9 The Crane

It's an essential piece of equipment for lifting engines from vehicles. Very robust and safe. Again, the crane had other uses.

It had two wheels on strong forward legs. Under the mainframe were two wheels on a pivot for directional movement.

It could be placed accurately with the front two wheels under the car and the hook on a solid wire rope, which was attached to a large hook for lifting even the heaviest of engines.

For our purposes, other uses became essential.

Dino was captured one morning on his journey to the parts department just before lunch. It was a Friday. Payday.

His hands were cable-tied behind his back and his ankles were bound. His green overalls used by the commercial fitters were the giveaway. He was the enemy.

The crane hook was attached to Dino's overall's belt, and he was suspended. Probably about head high. Dino was quite small in stature but had a mouth that a giant would have been proud of. As we clocked off from service, everybody gave Dino a gentle spin.

He was still mouthing oaths of death upon his captors. For the abuse, he earned an extra spin, just a little faster.

The lunch bell rang. Friday's ritual was a pint in the Queen Pub and a healthy bag of chips. Dino's punishment for being captured was, literally, suspension for an hour. No chips or beer for Dino.

We all returned safely from our visit to the ancient ale house, all in good spirits. On our return, we saw that Dino was flat on the floor motionless. His overall's belt had broken. We were stunned. The mood changed dramatically. Poor Dino!

His fall was well-aimed as he fell between the front-heavy metal legs, which could have caused serious injury.

We removed the shackles and checked his well-being. Thankfully, he was breathing, although bruised from the fall and slightly battered.

His eyes opened wide. He was going to thrash us all with bad language to match.

Hungry, no chips. Thirsty, no beer. Embarrassed but outnumbered. The uninjured Dino retired to the safety of the commercial area to plot his revenge.

1-10 The Broom

This can be used in many ways, sometimes, it's used for sweeping up, but that is boring. The same Dino again was selected for special treatment. He was guilty of breathing in a public place.

Ambushing him on the risky task of collecting spares from the joint stores' area was easy. The logistics had already been worked out. Dino was only five feet and six inches. Most doors are well over six feet tall. These were proper doors, not the monkey board that you get today.

Again, Dino's feet were tied. The broom was inserted, not maybe where you were thinking, but a little higher. It went through the arm of his overall and behind him and out the other arm, holding his arms out straight.

The two doors to the parts department were opened and the broom head-wedged behind the first door. Dino and the broom handle were now lifted in position with the handle now suspended above the second open door.

The door was now locked in this position, so no door movement was possible. He looked crucified. This meant anybody, if they so wished, could inflict torture on the poor soul.

His nose was greased by our most junior apprentice. His bootlaces were removed and cut into short strips. His left boot was sprayed a beautiful yellow, the other a striking cream with a bolt drilled through the heel and a nut fitted to secure it firmly.

After an hour or so, suspecting foul play, his foreman came to his aid. His first question was, "What are you doing up there?" This was followed by, "Where did you get the broom from?"

He was released and ushered away by his foreman along with the parts he was to collect.

1-11 Dino's Revenge

It was never proven, but he was the main suspect. Things happened to Dino mainly because he was mouthy.

Because he seemed always to be outnumbered, he could not fight back, so covert methods occurred. We suspected him as his start time was eight in the morning.

On the day in question, we were told he was seen before six o'clock. Very unusual! Our workshop had no life until just before eight when all the staff rolled in. Bumble's metal cup, his trademark, was screwed to the bench with a big self-taping screw.

Four toolboxes had their locks super-glued resulting in the need to cut them off. Three other toolboxes were full of grease and the foreman's daybook pages had been removed and burnt. Town's big screwdriver now had a right-angle bend halfway down. Barney had a Philips screwdriver that was ground flat on the end.

The General Manager got to hear of the latest chain of events. He had overlooked many previous actions.

Later that day, both the truck and car foremen were summoned to a meeting to discuss these issues.

It was felt that the time for horseplay was over as someone may well get hurt. More to the point, they also felt that the lost manhours were affecting production. Notices went up both in the car and commercial service so we had to behave for a while.

1-12 Friday Nights

Every Friday, fully funded, many technicians attended a gathering. This was the starting location.

Generally, no cars were involved. As an apprentice, to be invited was an honour. Lots of Daves were there, and the gathering was growing in size.

The objective was clear. Consume alcohol, and have a good time.

No police involvement was required, although they tried to help sometimes. About six pubs in, Bumble gave an attractive young lady a gentle pinch on her bottom. She turned around and slapped Shep, who was behind her but was not guilty of the incident. Six pubs in, three contestants were doing poorly. They had drunk too much too quickly.

So, the next stop was across the road from the London Tavern. It was the Railway Hotel, where we met some friends. They were a crowd of ladies from The Lyon's "Whip It Quick" restaurant and coffee bar in town.

They could clear your cups before they got anywhere near the saucers. By now, it was after ten in the evening. A lot of the folks were dating, and I believe some went on to marry.

Sam 48 (My Way)

I have to miss some of the story, maybe I forgot, maybe I didn't.

Cars would be retrieved from a resting area, and a convoy would head to the new food outlet, this being on the M2. The twenty-four-hour Farthing Corner diner was the new à la carte feeding ground for the mixed mob. Anything greasy was swallowed and then it was back to home.

Saturday was always a slow starter at the garage. Sometimes people were no-shows but had been clocked on.

As with most things, this gradually came to an end with people getting older or even worse, getting married.

Chapter 2

The Pits Construction

2-1 This is just a hole in the floor, or is it?

The pit is a way to access the underside of a vehicle to carry out maintenance, repairs or inspections.

It has largely been replaced, in recent times, by versatile two-post lifts. Our pit had four steps going down at each end. It was also four vehicles wide. The two outer bays ran the whole length of the vehicles.

The two centre bays had only access to the front of the vehicle once the pit boards were removed.

Approximately five feet deep throughout, a fluorescent light covers it all the way. These also cover the vehicles' whole length on the outer bays. The width of the pit covering boards is about four feet.

Given this, the vehicle has a six-inch safety clearance for the wheels on each side of the pit boards. Once the two-inch-thick boards are refitted correctly, it is a safe walking area and can also support vehicles.

Now, vehicles can be driven over this solid area, one hopes, without any trauma, but just wait and see.

2-2 Pit Boards

As I said earlier, the pit board was very safe, almost like a solid wooden floor.

However, there can be an issue at one end when accessing the pit—climbing down the steps. Boards need to be removed. Between four for slim people and six for the larger ones or for large vehicle parts. The runners that hold the board are sturdy two-inch angle irons built into the concrete during construction. All the boards fit perfectly into this frame. They were made of proper hardwood, were oily and very heavy. To be able to use the steps, four or five boards over the steps needed to be removed.

Very often, these are not replaced as the next job may require the same access under the vehicle. The norm was to leave the boards to one side.

2-3 Enter Jim

Jim was a would-be rally driver. His car, the Zephyr, had an exhaust blow, and Jim gave an impressive noisy wheelie! The Zephyr was not on the safe edge of six inches but on these heavy pit boards.

Jim reversed his pride and joy into position with one more big noisy rev-up for all to enjoy. The back boards shot back like matchsticks and the front boards gathered pace, trying to catch up. The whole lot of twenty-four boards were now in the pit, leaving just two in the front. The car had tried to join the boards in the pit.

With the vehicle subframe and the wheel dangling, a red-faced Jim emerged from it.

WHOOPS!

There was a lot of discussion on how to recover this heavy vehicle. All the technicians and apprentices were summoned along with the cleaner and the foreman.

Finally, placing ourselves in strategic positions under it, all of us lifted in unison. Upwards and then sideways. The Zephyr was out.

2-4 Underground Football

It wasn't yet an international sport, but many matches were played by two teams of two.

At the far ends were the goals. The ball was an orange shade and heavy-duty plastic, so it was quite durable.

The ball lived in the corner of the pit and was, therefore, a constant reminder for a game on. The ball was part of the furniture, it had been born, I suspect, in the pit. It had a raised, plastic pimple pattern, which of course would gather any oily residue, adding to its weight.

One major issue was the five-foot-deep pit, with only a six-inch clearance for a vehicle, and I was five feet ten inches tall. Ouch!

We quickly learned to kick the ball without lifting our heads or leaning back.

When a goal was scored, there was a thud against the concrete wall at the end, which could be heard all around.

Time was called over the intercom, the foreman asking when work was going to start! Inconsiderate fitters who may have been working on the centre bays were obstructions that enhanced the action.

2-5 Oily's Baccy

Oily Burt, an older character, was so named as everything he owned was covered in oil. His shoes appeared damp and glossy; his overalls almost stood up on their own, and his hands were never clean. He had suffered a hard life and it showed. He still had nine of his own teeth, three of which were black.

Oily used to smoke roll-ups. He was known to have half an ounce of tobacco, which had to last the whole week.

One of Oily's roll-ups would last just a few seconds. The tobacco strands were laid almost end to end and the Jolly Rizla paper, therefore, had no bulk. We called the smokes, racehorses. Lit and gone.

His task was to change the oil in cars that were in for service. One day, he was sitting on the second step, rolling a fag. Oil was draining into its bucket, and as most of the oil was out, its angle reduced and moved towards Oily's lap.

Under normal circumstances, this would not have fazed him, but disaster! Oil filled his baccy tin. He had lost his focus for just a few seconds.

Almost in tears as it was a Tuesday, and he didn't get paid until Friday, Oily tried to dry the tobacco on a newspaper.

Drying the tobacco on a newspaper did not work. The tobacco came in Rizla paper, so the oil had immediately soaked into it.

Once he ignited it, we feared for Oily's life. The whitish racehorse. It just seemed to burst into a flame.

Grovesie, I and a couple of the techs did chip in and bought him some fresh tobacco. He became our mate for life.

2-6 Mini Skirts

The 1960s were a time for fashion. Some of the girls in the Accounts department were very presentable.

This was the time that Mary Quant introduced the miniskirt.

Generally, the girls were advised to keep well away from the lower class, the occupants of the garage, in fact, anybody who wore overalls.

There was a need for one of the Accounts juniors to collect various documents from the service departments. The route for the unsuspecting lady was a journey from the foreman's office and past the pit.

From there, the next stop was to continue to the spares' hatch at around 9 a.m. each weekday. This was to collect the previous day's invoices and such things from there. Some of the girls hated this trip while others were a little more adventurous.

When unused, the pit boards were pushed together for safety reasons. There were no gaps between the boards. Therefore, almost no light filtered in from above.

The garage was unusually quiet as most of the lads were in the pits. It was a good time of the day and could, hopefully, get even better.

Paddy was attempting to try to make a gap between the boards. Andy, the foreman, was distracting Vivien by calling her back. He had found some additional paperwork.

Vivien was talking to Bob beside the end pit for a good minute. The talk was all about a lot of nothing.

All went wrong for Paddy when the screwdriver he was using as a lever, slipped and gashed his thumb.

Screams of pain came from the pit. A plaster was all that was needed for the big baby. Vivien cut short her conversation and returned to collect the files.

Word went around the Accounts staff in no time at all. Their manager announced that the pit was a dangerous place, and for the girls to avoid the danger of the pits. To take extra care.

Falling into the pit is dangerous, but also for modesty to remain intact. Extra distance should be given when walking past to avoid viewing hazards, or longer skirts should be considered.

2-7 Fire Down Below

Part of the car service was cleaning the filter within the petrol pump—every time, every service.

It was, I think, the fourth item on the check sheet. We missed this at the time but tried to play catch up.

Usually, it was done at the outset of the service, but on this occasion, it was left until the checklist was completed. Satisfied that all was now complete, the car was considered ready for the road test.

Bob, the tester, came and started the vehicle. Before I could shut the bonnet, the starter motor caught fire.

The petrol that had been released with the petrol pump's glass bowl being cleaned, had dropped directly on the starter motor. Normally, evaporation within a few minutes removes any issues.

When electricity was applied, the starter caught fire. Bob, the road tester, panicked and jumped from the car and leapt down the pit steps with the bright yellow seat cover. He was in full fireman mode with a cunning plan to smother the flames.

Me, being diligent and of a quick mind, grabbed the nearest fire extinguisher, aimed and emptied it. The fire was out, no damage done, but Bob emerged from the pit, resembling a flour grader.

I was called a silly fellow or something similar. The place was in total uproar. A memo went up on the notice board about my quick actions, which had averted a serious situation.

Bob did not like me or the notice. I wonder why!

2-8 The Bell

We were paid at the rate of a time and a half for Saturday mornings, so we tried to top up our meagre pay with extra hours.

It was also a half-day, and we did not have a full workload. It was a good time for a tidy-up and a good clean-up.

The hours of work were 8 a.m. to 12 noon. By eleven, all was clean and tidy-ish. So as not to disturb the peace, all and sundry would disappear into the pit—a sacred place where the reflections of a good week's work were discussed along with Town's adventures (in his mind) when he was in India and was attacked by the natives of Punjab.

Town never even had a passport. In fact, I am sure he had never left Kent, except in later life, on the cross-channel ferry.

His adventures were drawn using a screwdriver on the greasy, black floor covering that lived on the pit floor. Each week, the story got bigger and better. This week's edition was the *wadi* (dry riverbed) and the herd of local camels.

The sketches of the conflict on the floor covering were complex, with cannons, flagpoles and tents for the fusiliers. Then, the landing strip for the airship and it went on, expanding weekly. If it were discovered in 2000 years' time, it would be a very famous floor painting of the mechanic era.

Mr Ron, one of our directors, just happened to be walking past and through the garage with his stick. He would do this occasionally while admiring his domain.

Not quite sure of the almost silence, Mr Ron stopped. There should be some noise from a garage on a Saturday morning. Mr Ron was in for a shock.

The tale was cut short at 11.55 a.m. The bell rang for washing time, five minutes before clocking off from work. The pit boards erupted with shouts, whooping, squealing and the sound of falling wood from the pit boards landing on the ground. Twenty or so souls emerged from the pit in five seconds flat, leaving just the hole in the floor.

After the initial shock, Mr Ron was amazed at what he witnessed. Fortunately, his heart did last many more years.

After wash time and before the crush to escape for the weekend, we put all the pit boards back in place. There was then the usual free-for-all as all the staff tried to be the first to clock out.

Chapter 3

Accidents

3-1 First Free Service of a New Ford Zephyr

A new Zephyr was being serviced by Ray the Bean.

Four vehicles a day, five days a week and two on Saturdays. Customers were invited to wait in the reception area as the service bay was visible from there. Mr Saphire was the proud owner of this new Zephyr which had just about 500 miles on the clock.

Tranquility was broken by a very loud crunching of metal, glass and plastic. The Zephyr had taken a plunge south from the lift, a drop of some eight feet, assisted mainly by gravity. Clearly, the vehicle was somewhat shorter in length now than when it was designed for production.

Mr Saphire was speechless.

Our Service Manager appeared from nowhere and offered a beverage to calm him down. Mr Saphire was given a demonstrator vehicle to use for the weekend.

It was obvious they could not charge for the servicing—although they would have liked to. The vehicle was replaced free of charge with an identical replacement manufactured to the original length.

The only fatality during this event was Mr Saphire's clay pipe. Unfortunately, it did not survive the flight. Mr Saphire took this very well in the end.

More apologies were offered by our Service Manager. As promised, a brand-new, identical Zephyr was delivered to Mr Saphire at the beginning of the following week.

After a lengthy stay in the body shop, the flying Zephyr was advertised as a demonstrator. This had one previous owner and, with low mileage, was a wonderful bargain. Of course, once it was fixed, there was no mention of its previous flight.

The nearly new Zephyr was resold to a very happy customer who was pleased with the discount.

3-2 The Old Hill

Local to our garage was a steep hill that was busy even at the time. For better or worse, it is now a dual carriageway.

This major road has issues but is still undergoing major surgery. It was a road-test route for anything requiring a vehicle to do more than 50 mph. The old hill had a two-way traffic road with two white lines somewhere near the middle. Trucks crept up the hill shrouded in black smoke with top speeds below 10 mph on some occasions.

The tailback numbered dozens of vehicles attempting to cross the North Downs. Coming down was different. Speed could be gained by gravity as well as by the 1600 cc engine in full swing.

The average car in the '60s maxed out at 70 mph. The car in question had a tow bar and was used for family vacations. It also had a proud GB sticker. Bolt-on, extended wing mirrors were fitted to each front wing for the driver to see behind the vehicle when the caravan was attached.

Leaves and debris always gathered on the hill, so cleaning it was always an issue. We had a regular hill cleaner, short, fat, happy and regular. He always faced the oncoming traffic. Except one Tuesday.

We came down the hill, and Mr Cleaner was on the wrong side. The cart was nudged by the extended wing mirror, and the mirror was now fit to be swept up with the rubbish.

The cart's handle hit the cleaner's butt, and he did a full forward roll. We did an emergency stop and walked back 100 yards up the hill, expecting death, injury or other issues. We wondered which part of this character's body the cart handle had entered.

Bob, as he introduced himself, apologised for being in the wrong lane. The only damage was to his trousers, which were ripped and his whitish underwear was exposed for all to see.

After fitting a new mirror back at the base, we returned and checked him out. He and his cart were all in good working order.

He appreciated the cakes we gave as a memento of the memorable event.

3-3 The Horse

Rolly The Egg, was a senior tester, very thorough and dedicated to his job. Rolly had little hair, but he brushed the strands carefully on many occasions, getting it into a place that suited his taste.

Of course, he loathed being called The Egg, so Rolly The Egg was his assigned handle. A Lotus Cortina in those days was a fast car and always fun to drive. Our road-test route was set and The Egg was diligently testing the car when, from nowhere, a horse appeared.

After the bang of impact, The Egg's first sight of this animal was in mid-air upside down via the interior mirror.

Shaken by what had occurred, Rolly stopped the car and got out. The horse was not injured. It got to its feet, shook itself and galloped off. We spent the next hour or so looking for its rider, that is, its jockey but with no luck. The police were called, who then explained that it was the third time this horse had escaped in the last week or so.

A new windscreen and door pillar were needed. They were welded and painted within hours and the job was as good as new.

The customer's car was returned, all repairs completed, and the customer was told that replacing the windscreen had been necessary as it was damaged during road testing, all at our garage's expense.

3-4 Aluminium Housing

Some of the fuel pump housings are made of aluminium. This is a light material with many uses.

In the motor trade, weight is always an issue, so aluminium is often preferred to steel. We use an acid-based, powerful cleaning solution for cleaning the fuel pump components. It smells awful and is very corrosive, and care must certainly be taken with this product. We keep it outside in a covered but open area, next to a railway cutting.

Once a subject is deployed to our section of the company, the fun can begin. We had a new victim. We will call him Duffer, a young and eager-to-please lad, but green. We did not ask him to drink the solution, but I believe he would have if asked. Instead, we gave him the official safety instructions necessary for using this product.

A fuel pump was stripped and covered in heavy red paint. During refurbishment, the paint must be removed. We have options, such as wire wheels, paint stripper, also bead blasting.

The duffer elected the easy way out. He put the aluminium housing into the paint stripper. All the aluminium parts were removed from his basket without his knowledge. Overnight, the paint stripper did its work. Water was draining from the basket before it could wash it.

There was no main housing left. The technician said he should not have left it in the solution. He was told that the acid had dissolved it overnight.

With trepidation in his voice, he told me of his ordeal.

I made him stand in the silly corner before producing the same vanished housing. I think he said, "That's not funny," but everybody fell about laughing.

3-5 Forklift

This very heavy, useful machine can be a challenge to drive.

Today, we have specialist driving courses for these beasts, but in those days, you just did your best.

Our fork truck had the rear wheels to steer, and the front wheels were fixed and straight. So, this had a feature that was exactly the opposite of a conventional road vehicle.

Stevo took the challenge of driving the fork truck along a narrow path to pick up some empty wooden engine boxes.

At twice the required speed, he corrected the steering, but of course, in the wrong direction. His quick reaction was to jump clear and save any serious injury to himself or worse. The now giddy forklift went where it was aimed, but not directed—to the right, not the left.

The forklift was not so lucky after its eight-foot fall; the rear axle was now detached. Its landing spot was a concrete pad, and the crater of impact where it came to rest still exists.

So very lucky that no one got injured.

3-6 The Forklift's Second Appearance

The Truck Service Manager, we called him Meat Ball, was sitting in his office.

This was a unique event in itself as he was generally visiting the library in town to exchange his books.

Crackers was driving the fork truck to lift a commercial engine with a heavy chain attached to the forks. And Crackers did exactly what Stevo had done—steered in the wrong direction. Wanted to go right, went left.

The two forks speared the rear wall of the Service Manager's office. Crackers panicked and raised the forks. There were two-yard-high vents in the office wall. It was only a stud wall but had two curls of plaster and insulation neatly in place just below the ceiling.

The Service Manager did not panic. He just sat there, whether in fear or genuine calm, we didn't know. He put his library book down and investigated the incident thoroughly.

Entering this into an ever-expanding accident book, he decreed that only trained people drive this beast in the future.

3-7 The Model T

One of the meagre tasks assigned to us new boys was to wash the company cars. A rotating list, pairing any of the first- and second-year apprentices was drawn up. So, Grovsie was my selected water baby. We had all now, even at the age of fifteen, had a few weeks of driving instruction.

I was driving around the company, gaining experience with many types of customer vehicles.

The car wash was not automated, a bucket, brush and sponge were more the order of the day. As we felt very damp after some hours, it was the turn of the company's Model T. The usual designated driver of this gem was not available but it did not seem to be an issue. From where the T was parked, it was a downhill run, with a hard left into the wash house. No problem, but the model T is taller than the average current Ford Saloon. The door frame of the wash and the roof of the T made contact. The vinyl covering was torn.

Gently pushing it backwards, the damage was examined. The T had the new sunshine flap. Glue was applied to the 12-inch split discreetly, and the vinyl rolled back to its original state.

Some shoe polish was added, and the split fully repaired, restored to its 1914 glory! It still remained undetected! I hope!

3-8 The Rewire

I will include here a very unfortunate incident that occurred on our premises, but it was not of our making.

We had a well-insured local contractor doing some electrical repairs in the office. Included in this were new fancy strip lights in our commercial showroom. This well-overdue exercise had been planned for some time and now was the time.

Light trucks had to be pushed around the showroom, and tall ladders were used to reach the high roof. Two rows of seven double lights were now fixed to the ceiling, and so were spotlights outside to catch the eye.

All the wall sockets had been replaced. In fact, the whole showroom had been rewired. This did not affect us in the least except for the contractor's four vans jamming up the parking area.

Finally, it was time to switch the lights on. BANG!!

The new lights were now on the floor, showering everything and everybody with glass. That said, just about everybody had gathered in the main office for this momentous event. Firstly, no one was injured. It was soon established that all power to the building was lost.

This, along with seven computers, five printers, a battery charger and the whole alarm system.

The senior electrician was summoned, and the fault quickly became clear. The main fuse box, which had been replaced, was new, and the wires had been crossed over.

The sparkie concerned was still shaking and muttering that he had thirty-three years of experience. He was offered a nice cup of tea, but unfortunately, he had blown up the kettle as well. Guilt was established, and another week of chaos ensued while the electricals were fixed.

We believe faulty electrical items from all over the company were wheeled in. They could well have been added to the disaster.

3-9 Moving On

I moved to the truck section of the company to gain some experience for my City and Guilds Craftsman's Examination.

This was a quick course and was all about trucks. Everyone was in heavy and green overalls. Not really for me, but I took it on the chin. Expected duration? Six weeks maximum.

3-10 A Loving Couple

During the second week in Commercial Service, we had a lively event, orchestrated by Holy Joe. He was working on an Arctic chassis cab, no trailer, as it would be just too big for the workshop.

We were at a work bay away from Joe when, all of a sudden, he was thrown clear, luckily! He had been sitting on the wheel when a large spanner fell down into the engine area.

The gear linkage had been disconnected for the procedure he was carrying out. The large spanner fell directly onto the two exposed terminals of the starter motor. Energised, the starter motor was instantly engaged, the V8 engine came to life and in first gear.

Joe was shocked but uninjured and now well clear of the truck's target. The bay in front of the truck had an ice cream van only partly repaired. Mr Whippy had been waiting for parts. It had been there for what seemed forever. The eight-ton tractor unit had a slender advantage—by about six-and-a-half tons. The forward motion of the heavy truck was impeded by the fibreglass body of the ice cream van.

This was only for a short time.

The "Kids Beware" sign now read "Kids Be". The crunch of fibreglass made one hell of a noise. The truck wheel was now on a metal wastewater inspection cover with the customary covering of oil. This truck wheel was spinning rapidly but not gaining great traction. The crunching noise continued.

The foreman attempted to solve the problem, but couldn't. He burnt his hand on the glowing spanner. To complete the event, the trusty hammer came into use. It was used to give the spanner a good whack.

Photos were taken of the incident, and one got to the local newspaper. With no names, though. Only the logo on the front of the truck. Satisfaction guaranteed. The truck had only minimal damage to the paintwork on the bumper. The ice cream van was totally destroyed and was swept up. The remnants of the fibreglass body were also scrapped. Insurance undoubtedly paid up.

We suggested a sign, "Beware! Truck at the back of the vehicle", may have been more appropriate.

3-11 The Villains

It was a dull day with nothing exciting happening, a light drizzle and waiting for the tea break bell to ring, when there was an almighty crash!

The roller door was dislodged and fell. The bay just inside this door had a commercial lift, which had been left about a foot off the ground.

This was not uncommon as sweeping up rubbish can only happen when it is in this position. What was uncommon was that the front end of a large Vauxhall had attempted to climb this lift.

The falling door did not make it to the ground but was balanced on the car's roof. With the engine still running, the radio blaring and water now escaping from this wreck, there was more excitement.

Police arrived within seconds. They had been in pursuit of this vehicle for some miles, we were told later.

Limping badly, the driver ran off. We watched him scale our back fence. He was heading for the stinging nettles and brambles. Not a good idea when you're in shorts. The front passenger had hit his head, and an ambulance was called. This looked a little more serious.

The young lad in the back seat was shocked but appeared uninjured. Garth, one of our stronger technicians, was told to keep an eye on him. "If he moves, hit him," he was told.

This was until the police dealt with the situation.

The young lad was terrified, he kept saying, "Don't hit me," over and over.

The runner had given up, realising the terrain was unhealthy and that with a bung leg, he could not climb or run.

The local press arrived, photos were taken and a statement was requested. They assumed I was in charge, so they were happy for me to describe the proceedings. I had just about finished when the Truck Service Manager came running across the workshop. Juggler The Small.

He had been in a meeting away from the action. "I'm in charge. Can I help?" he asked.

"No," the reporters replied. "This man has given us all we need."

We left Juggler The Small to it. He was gutted that he had missed the action. And we had missed our tea break.

3-12 Things That Fell Off

Technicians are only human, but more often than not, they get it right.

Sometimes things do go wrong, not often, but it's worth recalling these events. The most obvious are the vehicle hubcaps, or knave plates, to give them their correct title. When refitted to a wheel, the inner wire clip holds the hubcap in position. Some have hooks, but all can fail. I recently drove some distance on the M20, and they were plentiful.

Never a complete set but enough to make some interesting jigsaws. Wiper blades are another. The little plastic clip that, in cold weather, won't fit correctly. Correctly fitted in the workshop, but at anything above forty miles per hour, it just falls off.

More serious is the wheel. Commercial vehicles have pointers inside the wheel nuts. This wheel is very heavy, and even a small car wheel can be potentially fatal if it gets detached at high speed. Exhaust pipes are another frequent item. How many have you seen on the roadside?

Oil filler caps and radiator caps. Technicians love these. Should have fitted them back on, but, whoops!

Anything made of plastic prefers to lie on the road than be fixed to the vehicle. Undertrays are a favourite, battery covers, engine covers, even plastic mudguards from trucks.

This involuntary gathering of components can be greatly added to by vehicle loads—from dustbins, shovels, bales of hay, buckets, plywood sheets and, of course, straps for holding everything down.

I could go on forever, but you can add your preferred favourites.

Rubber things add to this collection. Tyres without wheels appear everywhere. Traffic cones in various colours, enough to go around the whole of the M25 twice.

I wonder how polythene sheets can climb a tree?

The list goes on.

3-13 Harry

Before he was employed by the company, he was known to most of the car fitters. Somehow, when an event was on, he seemed to be included.

He was just like the bad penny, always there. He also frequented our working men's club. His former employment included being a hospital porter and, later, a local undertaker. His face fitted the latter job. He appeared solemn and unmoved until beer was served. His name wasn't Harry but Pedro, so everybody called him Harry.

The serious bit was a nasty accident involving Harry somewhere in the Midlands. He was delivering a vehicle in the low loader and got sideswiped.

The wall, which he then hit, crushed the cab with Harry still inside. The updates on his well-being varied from being totally paralysed to various states of disability. It was probably a year since the accident when Harry was seen back at work. He was on light duty—dusting and polishing new vehicles.

This, of course, was interspersed with detailed accounts of his serious accident. Harry was never really happy coming back to the workforce.

He had explained the incident to all, so it only left the cars to clean. Retirement on grounds of poor health was agreed upon, so Harry was signed off.

But it was not the end.

Harry was, as I explained, a member of our working men's club.

Soon, and with much time on his hands, he became a committee member. It is said the badge makes little people big.

Harry did odd jobs at the club, fixing the handle on the beer pump and helping out on Friday nights. With his bad back, he stood on a table, changing a light bulb well above his head.

It was generally felt that the badge had fixed many of his injuries. He also became the club's representative at funerals. A semi-professional mourner. He had previous experience.

We believe he received a large note from the club for attending the funeral of each passing member.

He was generally invited to the wake by the grieving family, thus he was fed and watered. Harry has since passed away, but like many of us, he knew his way around a pound note.

Chapter 4

Tests and Bombs

4-1 Headlamps, Tests and More

Headlamps are now commonly accepted as a standard fitment on all motor vehicles. We found, to our advantage, that the bright light had other advantages. As we were encouraged to enter the National Technician of the Year award, this headlamp came to our aid.

The Insight magazine was issued to every Ford technician in the land but only to those who could read and write.

The monthly bulletin had a twenty-part questionnaire with four options for each question. One had to choose one of the four options and scratch out the answer, hopefully, the correct one.

All the information was in the magazine's content. We found a better way with our friend, the headlight, than reading the magazine. This was much quicker. All twenty ticks could be achieved with accuracy with the full beam of the bright light on the back of the scratch card.

This illuminated the correct ticked box. One tick and three crosses.

The ticked box was not always clear but the crosses for the wrong answers were. I think our garage had the highest entry into the area finals for the whole country. Our thanks should be forwarded to Lucas Lighting for making such a wonderful product.

4-2 Finals Day

I was lucky enough to represent the South East sector of the country in the Truck Technician of the Year competition.

This competition was open to entries in two sections, car and truck. After my apprenticeship finished, my employment moved from cars to trucks within the company.

Technically, at that time, cars didn't have diesel engines.

So, trucks it was. I swotted up the day before the area examination. My short-term memory worked well for the one day necessary to memorise the bulletin. I had a good result. I got the best marks in the South East.

The final was sponsored by Ford with an extremely large budget for this event. So, the reward was substantial for the effort and time spent swotting up. One year, the banquet and gathering venue was a place I had never been to. It was always somewhere I had planned to go but never did.

It was at Buleigh, home to many cherished vehicles, the motor museum. We had a wonderful day, visiting the museum followed by a superb meal. This went on deep into the night. Morning came far too soon. Our wives were treated to a leisurely trip to Southampton for the day, lunching in the Spinnaker Tower overlooking the Boat Show.

The twelve technicians who had gathered were supposed to be the cream of the country. I certainly was not in that category. Never worked on a commercial vehicle in my life.

We departed early from Southampton Airport. It felt as if I had only just gone to bed. We, the twelve contestants, were escorted by three high-ranked Ford executives for the trip. We were greeted by the flight attendant, a lovely lady, who must have flown with the Wright Brothers.

She looked to be in her eighties and had ear-to-ear lipstick, wrinkled stockings and wobbled on semi-high heels.

Gave us a fright when she spoke, as she sounded like a man. She was commanding. "Seat belts On!" she bellowed.

Fifteen seatbelts simultaneously clicked. We all sat in silence.

I did ask, "Are duty-free drinks available?"

Someone sniggered.

"We do not have drinks! We have not left the country," she shot back.

Silence again.

Bad weather was forecast at Daventry, so we were redirected to East Midlands Airport. Thick fog was over Daventry. It wasn't much better at East Midlands.

I have been abroad a few times and was unsure about this tiny plane. It approached the airport in a thick pea-soup fog. Thinking this could be the end of many Ford technicians who would be strewn across the tarmac, I thought of offering dear Annabele the only parachute.

I thought it would have been unsafe to be buried in a mass grave with the fossil trolly dolly. We did land safely eventually and were bussed onto our examination area.

4-3 The Test

There was a big black metal thing on a heavy iron frame. It was made so that it could be turned over safely.

I remember the instructor asking me if I could remove the Range Change. My answer was no. I explained that I was a diesel specialist and had never worked on commercial vehicles.

I asked if my answer was correct, and how many marks I had gathered. Not many. Thinking of the option with an air line and pressure gauge at hand, I saw the adapter connection. I boldly screwed in the adapter. The instructor was impressed.

The air line had something like a tyre pressure lever, which released the air.

Two things happened at once. I pushed the air go-go button while simultaneously, the instructor yelled, "No!"

I later learned that the pressure must only be increased from zero in increments of 2 PSI until the bearing moves.

Well, the ball bearing did move. At about 110 PSI, it received the maximum pressure available. Ball bearings travel quickly.

The instructor's screech of "No" and the thud of a high-speed impact with a display cabinet occurred at the same time. This confirmed that I knew nothing whatsoever about this gearbox, which I had told him earlier.

We did find the bearing, which the instructor refitted for the next victim to be able to remove.

The other 20 minutes of this test time were not wasted. We spoke about the weather, our scary flight and our scary flight attendant. By then we were good friends. My two percent marks, although never revealed, were for finding the bearing and spelling my name correctly.

4-4 The Banquet

Ford really went all out to put on a great show. Lavish scenery and the two technicians' trophies arrived in a Model T at the ceremony.

They stood now, taking pride of place on the top table.

My Managing Director and his wife were present. They were excited as he thought we had a one-in-six chance of winning.

There were six contestants. I had to correct the odds for him.

"More like one in six million," I replied, explaining that I had never worked on a commercial vehicle in my life. I was pitted against Ford Master Technicians who were doing this job daily and very well.

Happy with this, he said, "Then, just enjoy the evening."

This, we surely did.

4-5 The On-Site Presentation

Let me give a preamble before we get to the actual presentation.

We met this character while playing in a local football match. He was our referee for the match. He was short, probably five feet six tall, but muscular. He arrived on his bike. At the toss-up, the captains gathered. Hi Brov Yellow, our team! Welcome Brov Blue team!

He was fit and certainly looked it with his Kent Football Association referee's kit on. Not only did he look fit, he was also quicker than just about everyone on the field. Half-time came, and we all lounged about, getting our second wind and eating orange segments.

Brov was at it. Two tins of Fosters. Nobody ever knew his name, but he was known as "Brov".

Off we went for the second half. He was still quicker than us. I could see why he had a bike. I had never heard of anybody getting breathalysed on a bike.

Always one to take advantage of a situation, my MD would invite the local paper along for photos. We had a gathering directly after work to formally present my award for getting into the national finals.

All the entrants to The Technicians Programme from our garage were requested to be present.

Also invited were all the managers and department heads. They were also present. Our company laid on the food, and half a dozen of the Accounts girls acted as part-time waitresses.

There were probably over eighty people in total, milling around in the showroom before being called to order.

Our MD stood on the steps to the upper showroom and started his speech. We had an uninvited guest present. Brov!

He was a character of the highest order; he could sniff a beer from two hundred yards. He had been employed now for a few weeks as a cleaner or handyman. So, he was involved in the event preparations.

About a minute in, Brov started up. "Didn't he do well," he said, interrupting the MD.

The MD was quite stunned as etiquette had been breached. His response, although annoyed, was a stern, "Yes."

A few more words were said, and there was a pause for photos with my cup being presented.

"You should give him a pay raise," Brov chirped loudly.

Again, a hush went around the showroom. By now Brov's cards were marked. He was discreetly taken for another beer and led away from the proceedings. Now, with Brov gone and the excitement finished, the event rolled on as expected. His employment was terminated the very next morning.

4-6 Tail Lights

A new Anglia was launched and immediately became a successful selling car.

The particular newish vehicle had a defective light on the rear as a bulb had blown. It was in for fixing under the warranty scheme.

The customer had been raging and ranting for ages about the faulty light and the quality of the product. Everybody knew Mr Happy, the proud customer, and his ability to generate aggravation out of any situation.

He was still moaning when Glen struck the plastic tail lamp lens a lusty blow with his rather large hammer. The whole plastic lens was now in many pieces.

The orange lens had no visible screws. It was our first encounter with spring clips. The bulb was exposed and declared faulty. It was replaced and now worked perfectly. Glen had the satisfaction of going into the reception with the faulty bulb, complementing Mr Happy on his diagnosis.

The customer was still chirping some three hours later.

Another lens had to be sourced from a dealer some twenty-five miles away. Once the new lens was examined, the fitting became obvious. Push the wire clip upwards, and it locked into place.

We did feel customer satisfaction was served, and all were grateful when Mr Happy's visit concluded.

4-7 Bolt Bombs

I don't know who invented this explosive and dangerous device, but, hey, it was good fun. The construction was simple.

Warning! Kids, don't do this at home.

Take two half-inch bolts and a nut that covers two threads of each bolt, three threads are even better. For this game, a box of Swan Vesta matches is necessary. Break the three heads from the match.

Now, with the nut screwed onto one bolt by two threads, place the three match heads into the nut. Screw the other bolt into the nut but only finger tight. Now, the two nuts were holding the match heads in place.

Take cover, stand well back, and throw the bolt spinning onto the concrete floor. If all goes well, nobody gets injured. Most vehicles also need to be out of range. As the bolt strikes the floor, ignition takes place suddenly!

The expansion and heat from the matches can tear the threads from the holding nut with great force. One of the bolts is now free to move. It's on the ground and has nowhere to go. The loose bolt is now on a mission—towards the roof is success, through it is a bonus! Our roof had many small holes, a visual representation of the success of our efforts.

Once, we found a car's manifolds, which are pipes for air and exhaust gases, held on by brass nuts. These nuts are bigger and longer than the usual original parts. Therefore, a larger bolt had to be fitted to these new nuts.

Brass does not have the strength of steel, so all the better. As usual, we secured two bolts to this manifold nut, but the nut's capacity for match heads was larger. We could now get eight match heads into this device. It looked awesome. We decided to test it outside, which was wise.

The bolt assembly was spun onto the concrete pad. With a really loud bang, the top bolt blew off. The direction was unpredictable as usual.

It was also unsafe. Once the noise died down and things became quiet, we found the top bolt on a newish Transit's bonnet. Never again the big one!

4-8 Respray

Our body and paint shop prided itself on quality that was as good as a factory finish. They had just replaced the front wing on a Renault Dalphine that was a bright yellow. The job was excellent, but not if you weren't colour blind. The car was yellow, but the wing was lemon yellow.

It was sprayed a further three times, but the correct colour match could not be achieved. This Renault was parked out of the way, next to our workshop, while a decision on what to do next with the paint was to be made.

Somehow, during a dirty, oily wiper-throwing incident, an accident occurred. Wiper cloths were good at soaking oil, so they were good to get grease off your hands, the workbench or just about anything else.

They were recycled by the overall-cleaning company, so we had a fresh dozen each week. This was in the days before paper towels. So, as the week goes on, these wiper rags get heavier as they become soiled.

One of the wipe cloths had landed on the Renault's wing.

Carefully, and without scratching the new paint, the oily cloth was removed. So as not to own up to this misadventure, the whole wing was carefully wiped over with the dirty oily cloth.

We believe that this oily cloth had automatic transmission fluid saturated into it, which toned the paint down. The following morning, the body shop manager declared that the paint tone had settled down.

Orange transmission fluid and lemon paint seemed to have worked. The bright yellow car was released to a happy customer.

4-9 V8 Pilot

A very old but loved special Ford vehicle. One local owner had his vehicle in for a new exhaust.

The eight-cylinder engine roared with the exhaust broken away from the engine. The noise from the V8 engine was unique, but with the exhaust broken, it was chilling. When the garage staff saw the trusty V8 entering the workshop, the running board (a step on each side) was extended the length of both doors, so a ride could be taken. It was an occasion for free transport on these steps.

So, with five or six people jumping on the running boards on either side, it was game on again.

Now, with the horn blowing and no exhaust and twelve bodies shouting and hollering, it resembled a wagon train under attack in the old Wild West.

No wonder Mr Bathurst decided not to proceed with the repair.

He took his treasured vehicle away.

4-10 Brake Blocks

Putting new brake pads into an XR3i or Cosworth can be an expensive operation. Not to be taken lightly or given to an apprentice to just clear space in a busy workshop.

Mr Ron was one of the board of directors and governors. A lovely character. My first attempt to assassinate him was in my first year as an apprentice. His push bike, which he regularly rode to and from work, was in need of new brake blocks. What could go wrong?

I was supervised for this operation by Bumble who was not in the least bit interested. The blocks were fitted by me and tested in our garage, so good job the bike stopped. Bumble grunted when I told him that it was done. He was more interested in the tea break bell.

Mr Ron went home on his bike at lunchtime, taking the shortest route. Now, this steep hill was a one-way street. Gabriel's Hill was then a main through road. At the bottom of the hill, a level section of the road appears. It was reported that Mr Ron came down so fast, he would have got a speeding ticket.

Halfway down the hill, as he applied the brakes, both brake blocks shot out like rockets. They had been fitted the wrong way around. The rubber block sits in a three-sided sleeve. Nobody told me the blocks had a front and a back on those replacement components.

4-11 Mr Ron

The same Mr Ron had a new Ford Classic, a beautiful vehicle, but on occasion, it would not start.

We were called to his house, but we were asked to bring our Wellingtons. This was a routine our workshop controller knew well.

The ducks in Mr Ron's pond were often fed other goodies along with bread and bird food. This time, it was the turn of Mr Ron's ignition keys.

The Wellingtons were on, and the wading began. Fortunately, they were just about always in the same place, we joked, just under the duck.

Chapter 5

Innocent Victims

5-1 Whale Oil

    This product was rare even in the late 1960s. It was used sparingly in the motor trade, although I can't remember what it was used for.

    The true fact is, I can never remember it being used at all.

    We had a green apprentice, Hiram, a tall lad, nicknamed after one of the Harlem Globetrotters, the famous American basketball team.

    Our Hiram was always good for a practical joke and this day was no exception. The trusty shop bike was needed for this delicate operation. The bike was identical to the Raleigh Hercules version, which appeared gallantly in open all hours.

    An old, empty, steel five-gallon drum was a perfect fit on the forward-mounted basket over the bike's front wheel.

    A phone call to the manager at the fish shop, who was related to Dave (Bumble), our guilty person in question for planning such an evil deed, and he was more than helpful to oblige. The conversation occurred earlier and a planned course of action was agreed upon. The shop bike had a basket over the front wheel to carry goods, so the driver just pedalled.

The empty five-gallon barrel was put into the front basket as it had an exchange value. Hiram was dispatched to McFisheries, the fresh fishmongers, then on our High Street, to collect a full five-gallon expensive drum of the said whale oil.

The new, full, heavy barrel was waiting, ready for collection. As instructed, the Fisheries manager had knocked three holes on either end with rubber plugs covering the holes.

Two co-conspirators from the fish shop carefully lifted the barrel into the bike's basket. Hiram was mounted on the bike to keep it upright.

While the manager came out to get his signature as proof of purchase, the two assistants were able to remove the rubber bungs from the barrel. The result was horrific for poor Hiram. Fluid was gushing out all the way to the workshop.

It was later reported that the red traffic lights were ignored in Hiram's vain effort to get the payload home intact.

Once back at our workshop, the barrel had, at best, two pints of liquid still inside. Discussions went on forever as whale oil was almost £15 per gallon. Could we cover this accident up?

Water, most of which was still leaking from the drum, was just about free.

5-2 Hiram

Always an innocent victim, but someone had to be. This candidate was always in the wrong place at the wrong time. It was Hiram.

Our car park was called the orchard for obvious reasons—no tarmac but with apple trees. Our neighbour to the orchard was the Maidstone Girls Technical School.

Hiram's six-foot-four-inch frame was no challenge for the mass of Daves that attacked him. Clothing was removed, leaving the poor dude with underpants and horn-rim glasses—both necessary for survival.

The tallest tree in the orchard where Hiram's garments were now stored was next to the Girls School's tennis court. Much giggling was heard as the lanky, skinny, cold apprentice scaled the tall tree. As Hiram retrieved his clothing and dressed himself at the top of the tree, our General Manager received a distressing message from the head teacher, deploring this action.

On investigation, we got away with it as we left his underpants on. Much to the disapproval of the young lady students.

5-3 Hiram Again

Working was necessary on some occasions but it was always wise not to drop your guard. To avoid damage to the Cortina's fitted carpets, there's a rubber mat in its footwell.

When carrying out repairs, tools are often left on this mat and collected when the repairs are completed. A pair of pliers and a screwdriver were left on the rubber mat while Hiram assisted one of the Daves. He was asked to collect these tools to assist with the diagnostic checks on the spark plugs.

The Cortina was misfiring badly and needed serious care and loving attention. Hiram opened the door as the car was revved up, still misfiring. He attempted to collect the tools.

He was "shocked" and uttered an oath. Both the tools were wired to the plug lead and not the spark plug creating the misfire.

We explained he must have imagined it or that it was static. You need to wash your hands to reduce static.

Now, with wet hands, he had a second surprise.

Yes, another shock but with increased power as wet hands increase conductivity. The plug leads were disconnected from the tools, and I showed him there was no problem picking up the tools.

We connected the tools again to the plug leads, and, yes, third time lucky. A shocking experience! Poor Hiram!

5-4 Tom The Fossil

A character from a bygone age. He was of pensionable age even when he was born, I guess.

Sam 48 (My Way)

He did his bit for King and Country and after demob, became a handyman at our garage well before I was born.

We were expanding as a company with the purchase of another depot on the other side of town. Utter chaos reigned during this progression as the whole body and paint shop had to move to the new venue. The new vehicles were also to be stored at this depot because space was needed in the town garage.

The tractor department was to follow suit once the body shop was up and running. Any vehicle that had damages had to be transported. Anything else was moved in a convoy.

Five vehicles were dispatched from town, and Tom was in the lead car to bring the other drivers back to town.

Tom's driving licence was won in the war. I was told that if you could drive a tank or an ambulance, you qualified for a full licence. Tom qualified. I think he got his from riding a horse.

We set off for this episode with Tom leading the charge. We got up to just 20 miles an hour on the flat road. Turning right was no issue. His hand went out of the window instead of using the new-fangled flashers.

The road in question had a steep dip in it. Steep down one side and steep up the other. Tom knocked the car out of gear to go down the hill. Momentum was now lost, just for a few seconds.

Everybody, including bemused motorists behind us, had to stop.

Tom selected first gear, pulled away up the hill at five miles an hour, and onward to our destination.

On arrival, we were just about an hour later than expected, and questions were asked. Tom apparently had not driven since 1945 and was not quite used to modern vehicles.

What with sniggering from all the fellow drivers, we asked him when his horse retired. The horse was put out to stud, but for all concerned, so should have been Tom. Even putting him out to stud was going to be beyond poor old Tom.

5-5 Lost One

During the transportation of vehicles to the new depot, another champion came forward. Chas, a popular character with all. He was always on hand if you needed any help.

One of the damaged vehicles had been involved in a front-end crash and needed to go to the new garage. We had a two-wheeled contraption that was towed behind our van. This allowed the front of the vehicle to be lifted, so it could be towed, and the rear wheels stayed on the road. Well, that's what should have happened.

Attaching ropes to the damaged front-end was difficult. They looked secure though. The tailboard light was held on the boot by two, stretchy rubber bands.

Off went Chas, probably doubling Tom's top speed. Needing to turn right, he made the turn quickly. Just before the start of the downhill dip, he had to stop.

The car he was towing was gone. So was its trailer. Panic set in. Not only was the car gone but the trolley that was hooked to the tow bar wasn't attached either.

A swift U-turn found the assembled mass just around the corner. The tailboard light was still attached to the mass.

A helpful passerby told Chas that the car must have been driven into the trolley. He said he saw somebody running away from the car, so he thought the car was quite badly damaged.

The passerby was told that we had been called to recover the vehicle and that all was now well.

The trailer trolley was rehooked to the van, and its eventful journey to the new body shop was completed.

On arrival, the car was dumped at its designated bay, awaiting repair. The broken headlamp suffered during the car's rough adventure was added to the insurance estimate. A new set of electricals had to be fitted for the tailboard light before the incident was hushed up.

Chapter 6
Tricks and Gifts

6-1 The Sandwich

We can start with the morning tea break, a 10-minute break for swallowing sandwiches, tea, coffee or whatever.

The *Whatever category* is what we recall now. Ron, who loved his food, was generally one of the first to be seated as his lunch box was larger than most.

The story starts a short time before the tea break bell rang. Ron was out road-testing a customer's vehicle.

His lunch box was located, inspected and his honey sandwich opened up. It looked quite appetising in its original construction, but all was about to change. For cleaning steering wheels, we had a paper serviette, which was left in the cars as a freebie after repairs.

This serviette was just about the same size as a regular slice of Hovis White bread. Ron's sandwich looked healthy, and we had an idea for improving its texture. One of the new sterile serviettes then found its way into Ron's sandwich. It gave the sandwich more body as an extra filling. The lunch box was repacked.

The bell rang, and people sat quickly. It was quiet, all eyes were fixed on Ron. There was anticipation of drama, but to everyone's surprise, Ron devoured the modified concoction.

In a few bites, it disappeared with no issues at all, but the canteen was a lot quieter than usual. There was certainly a strange atmosphere, but no one was brave enough to tell Ron what had occurred.

Nobody ever did.

6-2 The Tannoy

This is not original, but they say the old ones are the best.

One of our more attractive Accounts staff would work Saturday mornings for a little extra pay. She would take her office work with her and also cover and operate the company switchboard.

We have two depots, and the loudspeaker system is linked to both workplaces. I phoned her and asked her to announce over the Tannoy, "Has anyone seen Tom Toe? Will he please call the switchboard?"

Four people phoned in and said he was just behind the Lone Ranger.

The better one was the Tannoy call for Mike Hunt.

"Has anyone seen Mike Hunt? Please call the switchboard."

The lines were jammed for a good half hour.

6-3 Our Chief Accountant

He was the self-appointed captain of the cricket team, upwards of six feet five inches and very old-old school.

Trained at the Dickens Academy for pole bearers, knobs, and I am sure, dry slope skiing. He was also an expert taxidermist, I guess. Could stuff anybody. These studies must have occurred before the war of Mafeking in 1899. On top of his hates, were anybody from the service side of the garage. He had forgotten who earned the money for him to count.

While I was paying cash in at the cashier's desk, Fullegar barged open the entrance door.

I said, "Good morning, Mr Fullegar."

He grunted in response. The two girls working at the cashier's desk were speechless.

"Thank you for the grunt," was my reply as I turned and walked out of the account's offices.

His hate for the garage staff was reciprocated. His appointed nickname was Split Pin. This was due to his long legs finishing just below his chin.

Our internal mail system was fantastic. It was collected from all departments between 4 and 5 p.m. when all were winding down, sorted and delivered the next day between 9 and 10 a.m. Sometimes, it took three days, if we were lucky.

Because Split Pin was made that way, he would get many envelopes formally addressed to him. Inside were a selection of, yes, split pins.

One week he was known to have received over twenty letters containing split pins. These arrived from all over the company. We had many depots now, and the word had spread.

Just harmless fun.

6-4 Redex

This was a much-liked product that was used as an additive when fuel was suspect in the '60s. Its main purpose was to add lubrication to the engine and, therefore, to prolong the engine's life.

Most people forget that a trip to the coast could be risky, as vehicles had no reliability at all. When we used to rebuild the failed engines in the garage, we used Redex on the new components.

We were told by our masters that it helped "bed the pistons" before the engine oil got around the engine. Once the engine started, of course, the combustion action burnt most of the Redex away.

To assist the new engine, a little bit more was added. Just a little became just a lot. What goes in, therefore, must come out. This, it certainly did.

I bring you to the present day—when a Formula 1 car blows a turbo, white smoke billows out from the exhaust. We had no turbos to blow, but we invented the theme and drama that was to follow for years. The more the Redex added, the greater the white smoke emitted.

Even engine oil can produce the same smoke but cheaper. Soon, the garage was dense with this unhealthy, pungent exhaust smoke. We had quite a pitched roof where the smoke gathered and as it cooled down, it descended like fog.

Nobody could see. The windows and doors were all opened, and we had an extra-long tea break.

Yet another notice was sent to all concerned to be liberal with the oil during an engine rebuild. It did not stop us though.

6-5 Radiator Blind

This was an unnecessary and troublesome gadget, developed by people in the aftermarket business. If the contraption was really necessary, the whole of the motor trade would have been onboard.

It was made in China, and the instructions read as follows:

1. Remove cooler.
2. Fit blond (should be blind) and replace cooler.
3. Fix handle in car.
4. Join cable to handle.
5. Join cable to blond.

This was our first dealing with an advanced nuclear power.

There were also no pictures of the "Blond". We had heard about oriental women. Hope they understand the difference between fire and fries with their finger on the button. The great Shepo, my mentor, had the hump when given this job, lots of mumbling about what a waste of money.

The job should take thirty minutes on a good day. We were well into the second hour. Blond was fitted to the radiator, and the handle fitted to the car.

The cable was a challenge, it was not just a cable, it was more like a necklace. Tiny balls were attached to each other by a link coming from each ball to the next. Almost like a chain. It was generous in length, I guess almost six feet long.

The handle had a length of tube that needed to go through into the bulkhead, so it stuck out into the engine's bay. It was to align the tube with the attachment on the blond.

Shepo never swore, but this time, he cursed the makers of this modification and anybody east of Belgium.

We had nearly got this cable through its tube when one quick tug with a pair of long-nose pliers was all that was needed. We had its length cut down to almost half, now well under four feet, but I got it. All of it. The whole lot. Shepo had let go.

I did not know what Shepo's reaction would be. We were both in tears as we had to start over.

I was now holding the four feet of cable with the long-nose pliers in my hand. We think this was one of the original Chinese whispers as everyone in the garage knew within seconds.

Andy, our workshop foreman, heard the banter going on and came to give advice. "Get a drinking straw, put the chain link beads into that. You should have asked," he said, wandering off.

We hate a smart arse. Within minutes, the job was complete. Sometimes, you just hate the foreman. Another notch on his voodoo doll.

6-6 The Box

There are some wide concrete steps coming down from the canteen and then back to the car workshop. At the bottom of the steps was an inviting cardboard box about a foot square. It was resting there.

In its earlier life, the box housed a fragile part about the size of an old, round headlamp.

Goose, being the first one down the steps, gave the box the customary right foot. An excellent shot. He would have placed the penalty into the bottom corner, bulging the net.

This did not happen though. The box that had appeared to be empty was not.

A cluster gear from a gearbox had been placed inside the lonely cardboard box. The weight of a cluster gear is greater than that of three bags of sugar. The box and its contents moved slowly forward but only a few inches. Fortunately, Goose had boots with steel toecaps on.

So, there was only a bruised ankle to go with his bruised pride. Nobody owned up to who owned the cluster gear.

6-7 Swaeooo

This event is dedicated to Andy Crackers, a fellow apprentice who joined just a year after me.

We had to walk into town on some occasions—cards for family birthdays and such. Other essentials included tobacco-related products.

Now long gone, F. W. Woolworth was just about the hub of the town and one of the largest, busiest shops.

We were forbidden to wear our overalls offsite unless on official business. Crackers' trousers did not quite meet his shoes by some three inches. This displayed his socks. The left one was mauve and blue, the other one, bright yellow and green. Fortunately, his shoes covered some of this.

Later, when questioned about the socks, he admitted he had the exact same pair at home. Us four cheeky chaps stood back in amazement at what was to follow.

In the centre of the town's largest store, Crackers took off. He lay down on his back and started spinning around. He was only using one leg. The gathering crowd wondered if he had had a seizure or worse.

The word Swaeooo (and I am not sure if the spelling is correct) was born. Crackers spinning, still shouting to his audience, "Swaeooo," over and over. As the shop's security approached to assist the poor fellow, he just got up and joined us, as we strolled out into town.

This event was certainly not rehearsed, but I believe our first vision of breakdancing was logged. The shoppers' faces were a dream, from concerned, funny and interested to where did he escape from.

No harm done.

6-8 Our Pet RIP

Tony, our pet, had a short life. He was won at the local fun fair by getting ping-pong balls into a fish bowl.

He survived the trip to Sugar's home. The fairground vendor did make an offer for us to treble our outlay for the fish and bowl.

No deal, Tony was ours. We now had a bonus. The stallholder gave us half a packet of fish food, enough to feed him for months. Could have been Toni, gender in those days was not a major issue.

Tony had pride of place on the shelf wall in our workshop. He could observe all that happened from his bowl.

His fame spread, everybody knew of Tony's arrival, but the no-pet policy was overlooked or ignored.

His short life of just four days in our care was tragic. He passed away. Sugar's attempt at resuscitation failed, the compressed air line into the bowl spun him like a top. He was pronounced dead and giddy at the scene.

We decided to take poor Tony in a procession to his final resting place. A route was chosen. We had a slight delay as none of us could march. We mastered this quickly. Standing in a row toe-to-heel, we slowly moved forward.

Six people in a row with straight legs, all moving in unison.

Some of the other mechanics caught on to what was happening and joined us. The procession had now more than doubled in length.

It was Sugar's duty to lead the procession, holding the late Tony's bowl on his last trip. The worm procession looked good. Twelve people in perfect step with not an inch between them.

The car showroom was passed, which is on the main road. Faces stared from the windows of the showroom. A car stopped; the driver was told of the passing of our fish. Many cars were now backed up.

This same driver asked, "Was he old?"

Sugar's answer, "No, just gold."

The zig-zag course now went past the Accounts block, and we could see that all the windows were full of heads.

The twelve front-runners were still just about in step, knackered but trying to keep shape. Twenty or thirty more tagged onto our cortege, making an awful din. The rabble at the end was dancing a conger. Slightly out of order like a little fishy.

Tony or Toni's final resting place was cubicle two in the Gents. A final flush and it was all over.

RIP

6-9 The Challenge

There were many Mensa-type challenges, and just about everybody wanted to try to be the best.

Butch, then a graduate technician, had one test that no apprentice ever managed. A large, strong, metal bucket was an essential stage prop for this.

It weighed just about five pounds or two kilos empty. Its real job function was to hold used filters over the used oil cabinet, so they could drain down.

The bucket was cleaned for this test and placed on the floor. Each apprentice was weighed and asked to add the weight of that bucket to his own body mass. This was not the challenge; it was just to see if they could count.

The apprentice was then invited to stand in the bucket. Strange, one thought. The challenge was then to lift the bucket up by yourself while standing in the bucket, using just the handle.

To this day, nobody has managed this.

6-10 The Second Challenge

A funnel, a watering can, a two-shilling piece and a whistle. A lot of money in the late '60s. These are the necessary props for this challenge.

The apprentice was to stand upright with his head leaning back just slightly. The two-bob piece was placed and balanced centrally on the victim's forehead. The funnel, then, is placed comfortably inside the jeans belt.

The game begins once the whistle is blown, with the chance of catching the valuable coin in the funnel. If you catch it, it's yours.

As the head moves forward, the coin placed on the forehead drops. It goes down and forward towards the funnel.

Just before the head moves forward, the full watering can enters the proceedings. Once the whistle is blown, quickly pour its contents into the funnel. The apprentice jerks as the flowing water is now washing his underwear. En route, the two-shilling piece is captured by the water flow before entering the funnel.

This is safe to try at home, my granddaughter will vouch for that. My wife had to dry her clothes in our microwave.

6-11 Eleven on the Calculator

Once the day's cash takings had been balanced, it had to be paid into the Accounts department.

This was a good chance to meet the girls and introduce them to a different way of life. I was quite good with maths and could add five or six sums of money without the need for a calculator.

I will call the lady Melanie so as not to embarrass her. I think she may still be my friend. One morning, she could not get the cash to balance after four or five goes, and the totals varied each time. She passed me the calculator, and I explained that she was using the 11-button incorrectly.

By pushing the one button very quickly twice, I showed her that there was an 11 button. I suggested that she had activated it by accident.

She and her friend Kathy spent a lot of time investigating the appearance of the 11-button but to no avail.

Three days later, I tried to put her out of her misery and explained that there were no 11 buttons.

She still did not believe me.

Still searching.

Maybe.

6-12 The Rose Bowl

This was a family heirloom given to me by my late mother.

I think the same item must still be on sale today, but I will describe its construction. There are three main pieces. A ball-shaped glass dome with a large thread blown into the glass. The base was heavy plastic, about three inches in diameter. This had the same thread. A rubber seal sat between both components. This was to keep water inside and prevent leakage.

The common and designed function for this was to preserve a single flower in water. It worked well; my mum kept a rose bud fresh for many, many weeks. I could not see the need for such an ornament in a garage, then an idea came to light. We positioned this on our reception shelf. It was covered by a piece of clean cloth from the rag bag.

Many times, customers asked us to tell them what we thought was wrong with their vehicle.

Maybe they had bored us for too long. Perhaps they did not want to spend on a diagnostic check. You had to judge the customer. If it felt right, I would remove the rag cover and rub the crystal ball.

It always had the same card inside. IT'S THE PUMP.

The MD was not impressed.

He reminded me of the huge investment the company had made in diagnostic equipment. He felt the income would be generated better with a printout rather than from the soothsayer's guess.

6-13 The Rag Bag

Along with our hand wipes, we had a rag bag delivered each fortnight by the company that cleaned our overalls. This was always good for some fun.

Dressing up time. Tony was always the first in line to sort the bag. I remember, on one occasion, he got a size sixteen dress out of the bag. On it went, over his overalls.

One small problem. It had a sleeve missing, but that did not matter.

Now Tony The Tailor, found a suitable arm in the bag—on a woolly jumper—and stapled it on.

The lovely green dress now had an orange arm, adding to the splendour of his black toetector boots.

His jeans were not necessary, neither were his socks, they would have spoiled the image. This catwalk picture needed public viewing. Tony set off around the company, but about halfway around, the boardroom window opened.

"What the hell do you think you are up to?"

It was a very cross MD, who was involuntarily paying for this fashion show—because Tony's hourly rate would be in question if he was identified.

Tony legged it, and nobody would ever reveal or say they knew who the mysterious person was. Some suggested Cinderella. Unfortunately, the boots would fit.

6-14 Grandad

Once a jolly, alert young man, now well-matured and in his early nineties, this gentleman was not my Grandad but of a colleague.

He was not quite housebound but used to live with his son and his wife, parents to Diz. Diz was a very steady, loyal and conscientious employee, just a year or two younger than me.

Both parents of Diz worked, so Diz would call Grandad at lunchtime to check on his well-being. The conversation was always the same.

"Are you OK? How's Billy?"

Billy was their dog.

Thinking excitement was needed in Grandad's life, I decided to make my own call to him. The call went as follows, "Is that Mr Holes?"

"Yes," he shouted down the phone.

Wednesday was early closing day. Knowing his son would be home early this lunchtime, I continued, "It's the Kent Fire Brigade here. We have had a call there is smoke coming from your roof. Please be careful," I said with tears running down my cheeks.

The phone went dead.

On the dot of 1.30, Diz's dad arrived home to be greeted by Grandad with his arms waving. He was, I am told, still in full night attire, white long johns, slippers and an unbuttoned dressing gown.

A full two minutes had passed before his son had arrived home. Grandad had gone almost running down the path to meet him.

He shouted, "The house is on fire, and the fire engines are on the way," at the top of his voice.

A few neighbours gathered in groups to watch the spectacle, either the fire or the long johns. Checks were carried out by helpful neighbours, and surprisingly, no fire could be found. Grandad was given a nice cup of tea by a neighbour while the investigation went on. Still no fire engines.

He explained how he had smelt the burning, and smoke was coming down the stairs. That afternoon, his son was regularly sent upstairs to check for smoke and fire. Diz arrived home after work, and the still-excited Grandad covered the event again. But in even more graphic detail.

The whole event was narrated to me and the others the next morning, I came clean and owned up. Diz collapsed in hysteria, as that was the highlight of Grandad's year. Grandad was informed about the false alarm and phoned me next day when Diz's mum was home.

He shouted and threatened death and the removal of certain body parts. Then he told me what fun it was because every day was always the same.

6-15 Our Rep Fran

A very military man and a former business owner, he represented professionalism. That is what we needed.

He was employed with no motor trade experience at all. My manager at the time thought that it did not matter.

Also, if I am honest, it was done to cure and improve our casual culture. Fran, as we will call him, took a lot of time to adapt to our ways. We got to him in the end.

Cauliflower collection from Planet Thanet was on Fridays. Our distribution van was more like the vegetable market stallholders' than for specialist motor trade deliveries, which was its intended purpose.

Bacon rolls from the town centre at 9.30 on a Saturday were also part of his duties. The canteen was shut on Saturdays, so the "Greasy Spoon" store was relished.

One Tuesday morning, I had him phone a Canterbury customer's telephone number. I told him that it sounded like a good sales lead and he best schedule it to suit his route. It was a telephone enquiry that looked good for new business.

I had "borrowed" from our switchboard lady, her company notepad sheet. On this official letterhead paper, was the number and name of the contact. I passed him this sheet. The contact was a Mr C. Lyons, who was one of their directors.

He phoned the zoo in question, and the lady answered quickly. Asking to speak to Mr C. Lyons, he waited patiently.

She said they had nearly fifty sea lions, but which one would he like to talk to? She would see if she could help.

She also said that the senior executive was currently unavailable as he was eating lunch. Fran smelt something fishy.

I was nowhere to be seen for a good half an hour.

By then, Fran had loaded the deliveries, filled the fuel tank and gone for the day. Speaking to nobody.

6-16 Our Rep Bobby

This man joined us from the company's commercial service area. He had good knowledge of our products and quickly built up good relationships with customers.

Bobby had a free hand to organise his day, which was good because he did not take well to instructions. He certainly gathered a lot of work for us, promising quick delivery that stretched us to the limit and more.

Every other month, we sent out one of our senior technicians with Bobby. This was his pet hate as he viewed this as spying on him, which was partly true. It was to give various customers an insight into our in-house actions, repairing their components.

Bobby was smart, he was pretty sharp also, but never wrong, he thought. Three of his sixteen deliveries were to customers within six miles of each other. All had their delivery notes or invoices paired to the goods.

Bobby would line up the paperwork in order of delivery. A smart move. Item one, a hydraulic cylinder, heavy and about four feet long.

Item two, six injectors from a heavy commercial vehicle, light in weight, in a box about a foot square.

Item three, a starter motor, again for a commercial vehicle, a heavy item, needing care in carrying.

The paperwork was correctly delivered, but here the fun started. The cylinder was delivered to the second customer. The third customer received the injectors. The starter motor was left at the first customer's.

Bobby had his company mobile phone, and all three had now called him. He was way out of the area but suggested the first customer collect his cylinder from number two.

He did the same with the injectors, and customer two collected from customer three. That left the starter motor, which he asked the first customer to deliver to the third. Confused he certainly was.

He had them running in all directions, but it all came out in the wash. He was not having a particularly good week.

Thursday morning, he reported that his company coat had been stolen from the van and with it the mobile phone. He was unsure when but had it on when he had left town.

I did nothing immediately other than gain some time to think. Bobby was in a flap. I asked him to give me until tomorrow to consider what action to take. We loaned him another mobile phone to tide him over.

Theft has its consequences, with awkward questions being asked, especially for losing his phone.

Mid-morning, the local, big plastic manufacturing company, phoned in. They had another job for us, but Bobby had left his phone there in his jacket.

"He took it off yesterday morning when we were playing darts in our tea break. I heard it ringing when I tried to phone him," said the happy customer. "It was on our coat hooks."

Bobby forgot his coat after playing darts.

Next morning, he was quiet, unusual but welcome. He was sent to the customer as the repair was now urgent. I told him they had two items to collect.

As he booked the job for repair, he took off his coat while inspecting a vehicle, he told us.

That's our Bobby.

6-17 The Gift

After I became a manager, I had a secretary, Libby, who was wonderful and was excellent at her job. She could also read my writing, which was a bonus.

Her only known fear was of spiders. So, a weakness in her armour was found. A matchbox was introduced to the script and a very dead spider inserted into the matchbox. The small box was enclosed in an envelope and sent in the internal mail. This was duly delivered by the postboy the next morning.

Libby opened the envelope with her name on it, and she found the matchbox inside the envelope. She shook the matchbox and then opened it slowly wondering what to expect.

Her scream could be heard from the workshop next door. This was where we were all stationed, so as not to be severely beaten. It took some time for us all to pick up the courage to return to our workstations.

Once the spider was found, still in the matchbox Libby had hurled to the corner of her office, it had to be buried in the outside dustbin. The thought of a resurrection from her office bin was too much for her to imagine. Again, we were warned by Libby of severe repercussions that were to follow.

6-18 The Non-spider

The coffee cup from the vending machine lay upside down on Libby's desk. In a second, the jovial mood in which she arrived changed. The coffee cup was an obvious concern for her.

After the matchbox incident, nothing was sacred. A couple of weeks had gone by where calm had prevailed.

My foreman has to take full claim for this traumatic state of play.

About half an hour went by with Libby still, point-blank, refusing to enter her office. To alter the stalemate, I had to bravely sneak in, kill what was there and make it safe. With Libby peeping around the door, I entered the office trembling and lifted the empty upturned coffee cup.

Nothing was under it.

Perhaps the wind blew it in, and it just landed there, my foreman said. His name was added to her death list while bad language was heard by all.

6-19 The Non-spider – Two

The coffee cup from the vending machine that was inverted on Libby's desk reappeared. It must have been a good three weeks before the encore. Thinking of the last encounter, Libby was not quite so petrified and gingerly approached the cup.

A scream broke the silence. There was something sticking out from the rim of the upturned cup.

Earlier, after emptying our Hoover, we collected some fibre and fluff. This looked like fibre and fluff. However, the suspense generated by the props department had manufactured a virtual insect's leg. This was of gigantic proportions.

It was a good inch long, thicker than a drinking straw and in a grey-to-black colour. Again, after a good length of time, with Libby still shaking, shouting and cursing all and sundry, it was my foreman who liberated both the cup and the fluff that had chased poor Libby out of the building.

Later that afternoon, my foreman was seen with the leg of fluff sticking from the corner of his mouth. Just finishing my lunch, he said. Libby's bad language was again evident and abundant.

She never did cut off the foreman's parts as threatened, though.

6-20 Wreckers

This was just a common name for breakdown vehicles. They are not the size of trucks you see today. Flat batteries were common, and our service van carried a large tractor battery for jump-starting. A tow rope was in frequent use. If they would not go, drag them in.

Then we had a Thames Trader, all graphics splendidly showing the company logo. It was famed for poor starting. To be sent out with this was taking a chance. If it stalled, bad luck, the vehicle it was sent to recover had to be started. On numerous occasions, the service van attended with a good battery to rescue both trucks.

The trucks were getting heavier and more complex. A larger tow truck was needed. Today, you see recovery vehicles with more lights on board than the West End of London has.

These specialist vehicles have very large engines and are generally purpose-built. We got a Diamond T. It was previously employed by the US Military. The crane was made of really heavy-duty steel and was rigid.

The tow bar was solid. It could tow a Howitzer, even a trailer to carry an army tank. Impressive, but vintage. I never drove this gem but at a reported top speed of 28 mph, well, not very quick. It needed a turning circle about the size of a football pitch. It was said to only do about six miles for each gallon of fuel.

One of the truckee fitters loved the challenge, this was to be his baby. Phil Goodwood, or PG as he was known, was a real character, and he dressed the part—tan boots, cowboy hat and a leather jacket with dangly tassels.

He had a full beard and walked even slower than the speed of the wrecker. A small van had broken down in a local village. It was just six miles away. PG was off, and he attempted to take the quick route, why wouldn't you!

This was the B212, very narrow, with a tight corner. Two hundred yards in, it was chaos. Everything had to back up, including the Diamond. About an hour passed. Down the A20 was the next planned course, all was looking good until the roadworks sign came.

The broken-down van was about a mile past this gang restricting access and putting out the cones.

There was a dispute between PG and their foreman. PG was getting back into the cab. Selecting first gear, he systematically flattened the long row of cones, now in his wake. After arriving at the stricken van, it was decided that recovery was not necessary. The battery loose lead was tightened, a quick thanks mate, and off went another happy customer.

By the time Phil had manoeuvred the wrecker back to the A20 road, it was now well into the afternoon. After getting back to base and parking, it was time for Phil's lunch break.

The water board did complain about the incident but had not taken the registration, so no problem.

Just a footnote to this is that PG appeared well after I retired for advice on some diesel parts. Yes, he now owned a Diamond T, which he takes to vintage shows. Same hat and jacket.

6-21 The Fire Alarm

Not a thing to be messed with, but again, we could have some sport.

We were notified that an annual fire drill was due the following week. This was to be treated as a full-scale emergency. Just to see how we would cope. We preempted this from happening on Monday morning.

It was blowing a gale, rain was coming down horizontally, and it was cold. The muster point was in the vehicle park by a tall wall, which was the side of our workshop.

Parked next to this were customers' cars, as parking was always at a premium. I guess it was just after our tea break, planning was already underway. One of the fire alarm buttons was set off. Bells were ringing everywhere. People were unsure—was this a drill or maybe the real thing?

No chances were taken, just about everybody was outside at the collection point. Many soggy people were present and hairdos were blown away.

It's surprising how cold one can get in the five minutes before the all-clear is given. The normal inquest on who set the alarm off was inconclusive.

Many had their suspicions, but we were innocent until proven guilty.

6-22 The Hanging

This was not for apprentices for breathing in a public place or an attempted assignation of the IT nerd.

This was to do with the lightning conductor cable running from the top of the Accounts office. It went straight to ground, which I guess was safe.

There was a joined cable of about twenty-five feet, which ran directly to the car workshop. This also had the desired safety feature disappearing from the roof to the ground. The suspended cable was the length of a cricket pitch of strong steel wire.

The cable suddenly had a pair of Hammy's old trainers looped over by joined laces. They looked lonely and isolated, but help was at hand.

Jim's size-nine Doc Martens boots were added to the hanging wire. Jim was on holiday, so he did not need them at the time. Tuesday, the trainers, Wednesday, the boot, by Friday, there were almost a dozen hanging objects.

One of the Accounts ladies had donated a pair of high-heeled shoes that were past their best. Shoes with shoelaces knotted were the easiest to hook over the wire. There were two wooden stars with hooks and again shoelaces to loop the wire. Nobody knew where these had come from.

There was a hot water bottle balanced by a plastic gnome. The size forty-two-inch black bra had only one former owner who declined to comment. Paddy's two, big, inch spanners were to assist the spectacle.

The weekend arrived.

By Monday morning, even more objects were added. Somebody must have climbed up over the weekend and secured the Texas flag with two hooks.

On Friday, we had discussed how to get two old Mini tyres in the game. We could just about throw one ten feet high, so it was not going to happen. We were beaten, someone had donated a pair of knackered pushbike tyres to the cause. These, again, were hanging by the adjoining string.

There was a rubber chicken, balanced by a loaf of bread still in its packaging. It really needed a photo.

The MD came in to work the following Tuesday morning. He looked on in amazement. After some five minutes of studying the artwork, he had seen enough. A message was sent to odd-job Jacko.

Jacko appeared in a white Transit with a roof rack. He then climbed onto the roof of the Transit and attached his ladder securely. All four legs of this A-frame ladder gave it the needed height to reach the cable. The first down was the first up, the trainers.

Jacko was smart and had the ignition key in his pocket. Next in line were the high heels. He was on top of the ladder when the vehicle slowly moved down the yard. The steering was locked.

I did not see this but was told it just trickled to a halt by the parts department's side wall. Jacko was giving the ladder a bearhug, frightened to let go. The apprentice disappeared hurriedly and anomalously after releasing the handbrake. Jacko was prized down the ladder.

The following day, a cherry picker was imported from our tractor garage. This came with two operators, hard hats and a selection of barriers to cordon off the area. Various owners were invited to claim their belongings back.

Jim had his Doc Martens back, but Peggy never claimed fame for her bra.

6-23 The VW Trade Launch

We were invited by the local VW dealer to the presentation launch of their new model. A good number of customers responded to the invitation. With absolutely no intention of buying a new car, we would look and see what was on offer.

A good start, lots of red and white wine and for the heathens present, some beer. A caterer was commissioned to barbecue burgers and sausages. Again, no fault here. Six salesmen, their sales manager and four or five ladies who worked for the company. The six vehicles on display had one sales guy per vehicle. The manager, of course, had the new model.

The older Diesel Golf had its bonnet fully open and had been meticulously cleaned for this event.

Looking at the engine on view, it was noticed that an EGR pipe had no retaining clip. It was noted that the missing clip could allow the pipe to fall off. One quick tug and, yes, it fell off.

Once the vehicle started, it produced more smoke than the barbecue. Everybody was fluffing around, one done, five to go.

The next successful target was the six-cylinder Scirocco. Quite an easy target. Remove the plug leads and switch the number five and the number six over. Just needed a slight distraction for the salesman. Done and dusted.

The very robust engine ran as if it had no issues up until about half-throttle. The injected fuel had not been ignited but injected. The throttle, once released, allowed the fuel to ignite. This noise resembled a machine gun in action.

The sales manager called close of play for starting the engine on this one also. Two seven-seater people carriers were on display, one a base model, the other, top of the range. Both sets of keys were not in the vehicles but were labelled and on the keyboard. Somehow, the registration labels had been switched.

The salesman, keen to chalk up a sale, checked the key fob and attempted to start the car. With some difficulty, the key was eventually forced into the barrel. Wonderful, but it could not turn, neither could it come back out.

One of the more senior sales team came over and tried, same result, many wiggles and wobbles and lots of tugging. It was stuffed.

It was then decided that the incorrect key was in the ignition. Incorrect key, correct answer. It, therefore, meant the other set of keys was with the wrong tab.

Chaos reigned. Those keys could not be risked.

Four of the vehicles proudly displayed were now inoperative. This was out of a total of seven. Well over a fifty percent kill rate. A good evening's work, but sadly not appreciated by all.

I will complement them, however, the burgers and sausages made the evening bearable.

6-24 Pilot Boats

We were blessed with having a contract with the operators of the Ramsgate pilot boats. My former boss and in charge of our section for diesel repairs fixed this one before my time.

Sam 48 (My Way)

We were asked to attend a pilot boat with an engine fault. We had previously serviced the fuel pump and all twelve injectors. It was never said, but it was suspected that the injectors were still at fault.

We arrived at the marine workshop in question. It was like Aladdin's cave. It had everything, including a twelve-cylinder diesel engine mounted in a cradle ready to run.

All of the cowlings' covers were off, as were the rocker covers and timing covers. They were right, there was a misfire.

Cups of tea were organised on the half-hour, apparently an admiralty tradition. I had seen what I thought may have been the problem but was a little unsure of the procedure. While waiting for the next whistle for a brew, I thought it would be wise to open the tappet setting.

The last cylinder was not moving in the same manner as the others. Then the inlet valve was not allowing air into the cylinder. The screw had come undone. It had only been tightened up but not reset.

There was a suitable spanner nearby, so I loosened the locknut. I set the tappet at the same height as the others, and all looked good. The cups were collected and washed for the next call of duty.

The engine misfire miraculously disappeared. Terry, their assistant engineer in charge, saw the whole event and was somewhat embarrassed. He came clean, admitting that he had, or should have checked the tappet clearances. From that day on, we were regarded as King Bees.

As we had finished early, we were taken for a routine test ride in a pilot boat. They were very quick, very manoeuvrable and hardy. You just felt safe. We were taken to the nearby dock and shown a wrecked pilot boat.

The pilot alleged that the throttle had stuck open, so they had no option but to beach it. This wreck had almost no hull as the pebble beach had done it no favours. Fortunately, UK taxpayers can fund this type of regular incident.

Chapter 7
Vicar, Vermin, International

7-1 The Vicar

One of our regular and well-liked customers was the Reverend Prewitt-Wood, the Vicar of Saint Mary's, a parish located in the leafy village just a few miles out of town. He'd been bringing his cars to us for years and depending on the season, would present us with a large bag of apples or, sometimes, plums from the vicarage's own orchard for us to share.

"We've been graciously granted a surplus this year," he would solemnly announce.

Nonetheless, everyone knew the "Reverend Hyphen Wood", as we referred to him, although some of us simply called him "Rev".

This, he seemed happy to accept! Rev was, I guess, in his late fifties and was the epitome of everyone's perceptions of how a traditional Vicar should look and speak, nonetheless, he was a really delightful character.

The Rev had one failing. He just loved to tinker with cars, attempting things he had read about. Somehow, the instructions got distorted during reading and application, and sadly, almost all the repairs the Rev tackled just fell short of the mark. This was the major source of him being such a regular customer.

As a result of his many visits over many years, he got to know almost everyone at our garage, so our reception usually suggested that he take his vehicle to our service area to explain his latest mechanical adventure.

He said he had a noise coming from the engine, which was getting worse. I would meet him there and patiently listen to his story unfold. He had owned this mature Rover diesel car for many years. As he approached the service area, we could hear him coming well before the Rover made an appearance.

Leaving the engine running, the Rev got out of the car to greet me.

Before he began speaking, I said, "You have a very bad tappet noise."

"Yes, I have just adjusted the tappets," said the Rev looking a little crestfallen. "I thought the engine was rattling a little and according to the Haynes' Motor Manual, adjustment to the tappets may well be necessary. The book said it is a relatively easy job, so I decided to give it a try. The job was not easy and took all morning and a good bit of the afternoon. I feel the manual has incorrect information as the engine noise is now worse than ever."

Our technician who would be assigned to this diagnostic check or repair was Gino. Before opening the bonnet, he said, "You have a big tappet problem here."

The Rev for the second time said, "I have adjusted the tappets."

Embarrassed, he was even more irritated when the workshop foreman heard the clattering and entered the service area, saying, "That is probably the noisiest set of tappets I have ever heard."

The Rev again said, "I have just adjusted the tappets."

One of the fitters from the next workshop where body shop repairs are carried out was passing by. Clive, a jovial man, did have some mechanical knowledge, and loudly proclaimed, "Strewth! Those tappets sound like a dozen mad typists."

It was just too much for the Rev, who snapped, "Oh, go forth and multiply," or words to that effect.

Well, actually, it was Clive who topped it. Always managed to jump in.

We all collapsed in laughter, including the Rev.

Of course, we sorted out the adjustments to the tappets in no time at all. We did not successfully discourage him from future repair attempts as his visits still remain mostly self-inflicted. We suggested his time may have been more usefully used mowing the lawn or polishing the holy candlestick holders. Clive, to this day, is known as the person who could make a Vicar swear.

I attend our local church regularly, but I have never been to the Rev Hyphen's abode, but I was tempted…

My regular attendance is for births, funerals and weddings. The temptation was to see if he would confess to his use of such industrial language during his recent visit, but how could he incorporate the word tappet into a sermon!

7-2 Dustcart

This refuse collection service is carried out by a gang of happy souls, just as you have emptied your bins.

All roller trollies have attachments to assist lifting, which makes their life a little easier. We have a congested and odd-shaped car park. There are always issues with someone blocking it.

The Dustmen, as we called them, no ladies at that time, could jump on the cart while it was still in motion.

We had ten bins, usually placed in pairs. The motor trade rubbish is a lot of cardboard from the parts, replaced and broken metal car parts, plastic trim and, of course, oily and greasy rags. This was before the days of segregating waste and recording if you used butter or margarine.

Our dustbins had an additional gift—quite a lot of diesel-soaked rags and paper and spray paint tins. Ours was the third of the five stops.

Our bins were emptied, and we put them away before they rolled down the yard. Generally, the dustcart is almost empty early in the day, but it was just about full that day. As it left us, smoke started to billow from the waste compartment and then flames. The fire brigade later informed us that spontaneous combustion probably caused the fire.

This is why they should be emptied each day before lockup. There was some panic as the dustcart had to abandon its mission. We did not want it alight on site. The driver agreed and pulled up out the front of our garage. Just opposite the petrol station!

He moved forward again and was now under the railway bridge, not a good idea. Finally, the two fire engines had the blaze under control, while the dustcart was resting on a grass verge.

7-3 Dollies

Enter a Ford Transit PSV Minibus, reported with the fault of running away, making it dangerous to drive.

We carried out numerous checks and repairs but found nothing seriously wrong with the vehicle's diesel system. The fault had occurred three times. With a minibus, that makes it unfit for use and rightly so. Not finding anything obviously wrong confused us, but we needed now to road test this small bus.

I thought a route similar to the bus run to collect children would simulate everyday use. So, I phoned my wife and told her that I would collect my daughter and her three friends at 3.20 p.m.

All went well, I arrived at the bus park and collected the eight-year-old children. They were excited to be picked up by a small bus, all got on and a lot of chattering was evident.

"Are you all strapped in?" I shouted.

Four voices replied, "Yes."

We took off for home. Only about a mile away. We were almost there and turned left into the road, which had speed bumps recently added.

We took the first of the four reasonably well. The high-mileage bone shaker survived this. Then it happened, thick white smoke emerged, and we were off gathering speed quickly. The second bump was getting a good bounce. I had my foot on the brake but was not really slowing the vehicle.

Now the smoke was coming in the back doors.

Travelling on a straight road, approaching forty mph, we approached the third bump. I looked in the rearview mirror and saw in mid-air, not the children but seventeen dollies. All in limbo.

My daughter screamed. My babies. My babies.

A snapshot of that moment would have been priceless.

Fortunately, the vehicle was now back under my control before the fourth speed bump. I pulled the bus up outside my house and said that we had arrived safely. Thank you for flying with me.

The dollies were salvaged from the floor, and everybody was checked for bruises or damage. The excited children were calmed down with a good feed while narrating their ordeal to their parents.

Once the minibus returned to our workshop, we found the fault. A plug in the rocker shaft had fallen out. A known issue that lets oil into the air intake. After this, we were wise to this fix.

7-4 The Nose

One of the directors was our appointed health and safety person-in-charge. We don't quite know who appointed him, but he had a badge and

Sam 48 (My Way)

looked very professional. He was a nice guy, always approachable, quite elderly and walked with a stick. Not to be messed with as he was part owner.

We were very busy, and the instructions to do a good tidy-up fell on deaf ears. Crisp packets, chocolate wrappers and stale sandwiches were disposed of and the rubbish bins emptied.

We have a rotary wire wheel, which has a safety guard fitted, so I thought there could be no problem with this.

Wrong. The safety guard was in place, but the machine had not been cleaned, certainly not in this millennium.

His walking stick, which was an essential assistant to balanced walking, had a second use. Under the surround of the rotary wheel is normally a dustbin, which collects all the waste material.

Today, there was no dustbin, and it had been absent for some weeks. There was a heap of debris where the bin should stand.

His walking stick was used to disturb this debris. Something shifted. I wondered what was lurking below. I knew most of the content of this heap on the floor, wire brush strands from the wire wheel, carbon, which formed the bonding agent, dry paint that the buffing wheel had removed and general dirt.

The drama was tense. Was it an animal? Maybe a rat? We were all concerned about what lay beneath.

It was the goggles, which should have been worn when using this rotary wire wheel.

Our rule of thumb was that with the surround guard in place, goggles were not required. Covered in crap and unable to see through the lenses, I was asked to explain. Thinking quickly, I suggested they had fallen, dropped by one of our technicians after finishing his task.

It became apparent that it was an impossible action to defend.

His stick made further inroads into the muck, and I was asked to pick up the safety goggles. I did retrieve these goggles, made worse by the injector sleeve that had been taped to them.

This mauve, plastic, six-inch-long tapered sleeve resembled Pinocchio's nose. All concerned chuckled, and then I was told sternly to take more care of the equipment. I immediately agreed, apologised for the horseplay and said that I will keep the goggle situation under review.

The nose was sent to the picket line for further duties.

7-5 Hydraulic Ram

A large, heavy hydraulic cylinder was in for servicing and had the main sliding chrome rod bent. Attempts to strip the unit by conventional methods failed. It was stuck solid. Under normal circumstances, it just pulls apart. Being bent compounds and complicates the problem.

Everybody had a view on how to strip it down, so we tried various options. None worked. Our workshop had very good technicians with many years of experience. Discussions were ongoing.

The cylinder was mounted securely in a vice, and a compressed airline was applied with a regulator. This would apply pressure, but nothing like the hydraulic pressure when in service. It still would not budge.

I struck the holding gland with a large hammer with the high-pressure air attached at full pressure. It shifted rather rapidly. The rod shot out with a lot of hydraulic oil like a rocket almost taking out the plywood wall in the next workshop where Paul, our electrician, was working.

Paul was not injured (the projectile missed him) nor was he impressed, but the oil covering on him stopped him from squeaking.

What the fudge! Where! were his comments, as some of the lads did shout, "Incoming," I was told after the dust settled.

7-6 The Pajero

This was a popular, robust vehicle, designed for off-road use along with family school runs. In reality, most were glorified shopping trollies, baby seats fitted in the rear seats. With fluffy dice swinging from the interior mirror and washed twice a week. It was obvious this one had never been off-road except for parking on the grass verge opposite their house.

Sam 48 (My Way)

We had received the diesel pump from this vehicle through a parcel carrier earlier. Instructions that the vehicle had "run away out of control" and the driver would not drive it again until it was fixed.

The garage that sent us the fuel pump gave us instructions to do whatever was needed to fix it. The pump was stripped, and no major issues were found. Once it was rebuilt with minimal parts, it was bench-tested.

As we suspected, the pump passed the test. Fit for use, so it was sent to the customer's garage for refitting. Our invoice had been paid before dispatching the parcel. Job done, we thought.

A couple of weeks passed when I received a call. It was the customer's garage, suggesting that the fault was still in the pump. Basically, asking if we could take a look at the vehicle as the issue was ours to solve and beyond their capabilities.

The vehicle arrived on a transporter and quick checks showed no issues. Many checks were carried out, nothing was found, although the engine oil was a little low. It was topped up and a local road test still showed no issues.

We were still puzzled as to what could be wrong, as generally, customers don't make up potentially costly faults. My decision was to give it a long road test after hours when the local traffic had died down. It must have been springtime as it was still light at eight o'clock.

I had my wife follow me in my company car to ride shotgun should I break down. We set off to the local village of Lenham, some ten miles away on this nice evening. All seemed well. We had stopped, and I looked under the bonnet. Still no issues. Happy to return to base, we set off back to the workplace. It was now getting dark, but still warm.

As I pulled into the garage, I felt a blip and then the engine settled back down. My wife arrived, and I asked her to wait while I checked under the bonnet. The Pajero was ticking over on idle, I left it that way while I was speaking to my wife.

The Pajero had a mind of its own. The engine speed increased. I watched and wondered. Faster and faster ran the engine speed, and it was still increasing. I ran to the vehicle and turned the key off.

The noise was now horrendous with thick white smoke coming from the exhaust. I stood well back. If the engine blew up, it was the best place to be in. A couple of the nightshift commercial fitters came to aid us because they heard the engine screaming.

We discussed the options. The fire extinguishers they had carried were in vain as there was no fire. This dispels the myth that there is no smoke without fire. Smoke there was. It was almost dark, but the white smoke hovered over the vehicle and was increasing every second.

The engine probably raced for a whole four or five minutes. It seemed forever though. The engine speed dropped and then came to a stop.

The dense smoke storm was higher than the three-story building the poor vehicle was parked next to. This cloud just hung about, moving slowly as a mass toward the main company workshop.

I went back to the vehicle gingerly and lifted the bonnet. The engine was glowing, so I checked the oil, there was none in it.

Locking the car up, I thanked the gathered commercial fitters for their help. Fun was over. The smoke cloud was still intact and had moved some 50 feet to the left. Not much could be done. My wife was panic-stricken by the events and wanted me to drive her home.

Some twenty minutes had passed with the route home needing a drive through a thick, white, smelly cloud. It was still moving slowly, intact and towards the centre of the town.

The following day, we had the task of explaining that the fault was of the engine running on its own oil.

It needed a new engine, and that was the original issue. Not the fuel pump.

7-7 Mr Dance

He was a character and a local farmer. I understand that he had bought the first Thames Trader we sold.

He always paid in cash—for the Trader, for his repairs, and somehow, he negotiated special prices. The MD would not let him into his office but would conduct business in the showroom, open to all.

Everybody knew Mr Dance. He was as strong as an ox but only just over five feet tall. There was a downside to him. He smelt like the same ox. There were worse smells. His truck, even when empty smelt of the sheep he would carry in it.

He was also stone deaf when he wanted to be. I recall a tale from my early days with the company.

Mr Dance's truck had a service on Monday, and he needed it back later the same day. Tuesday was a market day, with a thriving market in the centre of the town. He had sold some sheep, which were ready for profit, and bought some lambs, which were ready to be fattened up.

He was en route from the market to his farm. He drove past our back gate and the clutch gave out—fifty yards past our gate and facing the wrong way. He headed straight for our truck reception.

All that was left in charge of the vehicle now was Bullet, his sheepdog.

After he refused recovery and the costs involved, ten or so "volunteers" were seconded to push the truck. Someone ran back to base and rounded up a few more bodies. We were now probably twenty-men strong.

It was pushed into a T Junction and turned downhill.

Bullet had given way to Mr Dance who freewheeled onto the concrete pad to the rear of the workshop. This spectacle was made more of an adventure by the following crew of fitters running and waving behind him.

The next discussion was how long it would take. He was told we were booked until Friday. Off he went and spoke to his pal, our MD, and, of course, he then jumped the queue. This discussion took place in the showroom, everybody keeping their distance. A fitter and an apprentice were assigned the job and a new clutch was collected from the parts department.

Bullet was allowed from the cab.

Mr Dance was releasing the forty or so lambs to graze on the fallen apples in our truck park, called the orchard. Bullet was in charge, and no lamb was even looking to get out of the gate.

We did have a further issue when, slightly after lunch, one of our senior car technicians was called over the Tannoy, "Would Mr Shepherd report to truck control."

The truck controller said to him there were some forty people waiting for him in the orchard.

Mr Dance's next gem was only to pay for the parts as it must have been overlooked that the truck was being serviced.

Bullet had a reward of a sausage roll from someone's lunch box, his job well done as the cargo was reloaded.

All deep cleaning of the office reception was carried out soon after Mr Dance's departure.

7-8 The Segwin

This was a word I was unfamiliar with until I was invited to a Delphi presentation. About six weeks before this event launch, an invitation arrived addressed to me. It was in letter format but a type of brochure outlining their company plans. Of course, I needed approval from the MD before I could accept the offer. With the free promotion of our associated product, he was very interested and gave approval.

Just over six weeks to go. I checked the venue on the map. Somewhere in Buckingham. Two days off with pay, a good one. Plus, half a day to travel. All sorted. Their rep, Mike gave us a visit and told me their intended table plans.

I knew the other three from various training courses and also through the many phone calls we had in between.

John from Colchester. He was a wealth of knowledge and good company. Like me, he was the only one on the payroll.

There was Dave from Mansfield. He owned his business but was a true gem. Everybody knew Dave. He had a three-inch-long pointed beard from his chin. It was multi-coloured. By the way, he was the chief of the UK Mercedes truck-racing team. And of course, Mike, our rep. His job would be to try and keep us under control.

Sam 48 (My Way)

All was organised except that a curve ball intervened. I had a hernia pencilled in, but it was just a week before the presentation date. This was to be on a Monday, only 10 days before the Bucks' visit. I felt this could not be avoided, so I had the procedure carried out.

It was very tender down below, and I had my first week off sick in over ten years. I was given a sheet of do's and don'ts. Well, off work, it went well. No lifting, hands not above the head, no climbing ladders and so on.

I drove in to work on the Monday before the event, as I needed to catch up with the MD. He was concerned for my health and asked how long I would be off. It could be costing him money.

I explained that I had returned to work but only on very light duties. No lifting and so on. I asked if my company car could be swapped with someone who drove an automatic. The parts assistant manager's car was instantly seconded, and the switch was done. I explained that the leisurely drive to the presentation venue was now possible, again, game on.

I made it to Buckingham with no ill effects.

Mike, our rep, was concerned for my health and carried my suitcase to my room on the lower floor. Word had gone around that I needed assistance and special care should be exercised.

Time went on and welcomes exchanged. The new product launch was not too exciting. The team from Delphi were. They had practiced throughout the globe. The meal was excellent, and the wine flowed.

The Segwin was driven in by Barry. He was one of the more crusty people but a senior executive, so all paid attention. They showed a two-part clip on how this Segwin worked. It was somewhat like a moon buggy. A gyroscope kept it upright while the machine turned left and right, just like a bike.

All visitors were invited to take a trial in the hall, but Mike wanted to excuse me. I was not having that, and I climbed onto this contraption. It was OK, just like riding a bike. They then showed a short but challenging clip in the second half of the film. It was of the American President stacking it against a log in front of the White House.

They had a sectioned-off track outside, forming a figure eight. Probably some two hundred yards long. The time trial was rewarded with the winner getting a small medal with a large bottle of champagne. Probably forty or so agents were represented, but only maybe half wanted to ride. I just had to give it a try. I had sneaked out before Mike could intervene, and I was off. Just to see Mike's face was a treasure as we went by the presentation room. He was horrified.

I survived the whole figure eight but was a touch sore at the end, but it was worth it. Mike made me sit down for a while to get my body to recover, but no harm was done. The presentation was well done, so the evening continued as was the Delphi way. The whole of the presentation team was well at it, even Mike had a few glasses of wine. He was jolly. Finishing in the early hours, people drifted off to bed.

The following morning a healthy breakfast was fed to everybody present.

7-9 Delphi Call Up

We received notice for me and my assistant manager to attend their Warwickshire Training Centre. This was cleared by our company management. It was on a Wednesday, and a hotel had been booked.

Mike, our rep, said he knew nothing about this meeting, making it more suspicious. The two of us discussed all the events that could cause embarrassment to us all. We even discussed, maybe, they wanted to take away our agency.

Things took a twist the day we were to travel. Make sure you bring wet weather and warm clothing, we were told.

We drove to Warwickshire and were welcomed on arrival. Some sandwiches were made available. Then the UK Sales Manager appeared along with Mr. Delphi as we knew him, their Global Sales Manager. Hands were shaken and had cleared. We both noted their casual dress.

"We leave in ten minutes, so put your cases in the reception," we were told.

Still, none the wiser, we obeyed the instructions. As we boarded the minibus, I recognised two agents from the North of England. Nobody knew what was happening except the Delphi personnel.

After a lengthy bus ride, we arrived. It was Villa Park, home of Aston Villa Football Club. Delphi had a hospitality box for such events, and we were chosen by Mike, our rep, as a reward.

We were up with the Gods, food and drink on tap and a waitress in Villa colours. The six Delphi staff were cheering Villa on, but that did not help. Nil-to-Nil was the result. We wanted the Spurs to win anyway, but we could not offend our hosts. After the mass of supporters had cleared, a rapid tour of the stadium concluded the entertainment.

Back to the hotel for a good night's sleep. During the drive home, we decided we'd say the event was Delphi's launch of a new Zero nozzle. This kept the jolly up from the boys. The Zero nozzle was never released but reflected the score.

7-10 Invite to Germany, Luckily

The major franchise that we had for the diesel centre was a well-known German manufacturer. There were many stories, but I will try to recall one or two.

It was a family event, nothing to do with work, a visit to the war museum. A lot of the exhibits were of little interest to me, but I was fascinated by a German World War II exhibit.

There was a V1 Rocket, or the doodlebug, as it was known, on display. I was interested in how advanced it was for that age.

To my delight, some components had the part numbers. Clearly, this one had not exploded. I jotted the part number of a distribution unit on my brochure.

The following day, it was necessary to talk with the UK sales desk, and I asked the question, "Can you tell me, please, if this part is still available?"

It was in the old format of part numbers, which included letters, so the challenge was on. Their UK Manager was a good guy.

He almost had a British sense of humour for a German. A certain Mr Hoffmann. He phoned me back later that same week. "We have stock, there are three in our museum in Karlsruhe. You cannot buy this as it is now a restricted part," he said.

"And who is building a V1 Rocket?"

The word had now gone around the whole UK operation centre. This is the hush-hush factory with the worldwide research and development centre and training development. All service agents should be invited but only one per company. I was privileged to be invited.

We were collected from the UK depot by coach and flown by a chartered private jet to Germany. I think Colchester, Maidstone and Mansfield were again married up as we were in groups of three.

The research and development department was extraordinary. They were developing the self-parking car years before the concept was released. We were told not to announce this project as it was still being perfected. They had the machinery to check the depth of case hardening on a failed component.

We would say it just broke. They could tell you why. Very impressed. The evening was business, questions and answers, good input from all. The following day was a trip to the Mercedes motor museum. It was a circular building with no steps.

A lift takes you up to the top, and the walkway down covers, I guess, three miles. At the top were mechanical inventions before the motor vehicle, then the first Mercedes, just after halfway down was Adolf's staff car and many variants of half-tracked vehicles of that time.

Later, and more recognized, were the saloons of the '60s, with the good, older, faithful early Mercedes Trucks.

Two floors to go, current trucks and cars that almost nobody can afford. The last floor holds their Formula One Team's previous year's models. Nobody could afford them either.

Next to this exhibition centre was the Mercedes Truck Control Centre for production. We were invited by Dave from Mansfield to view this place as his guests. Everybody knew him. It was as if we were in the company of royalty. Gates were opened, everybody greeted him fondly and all knew his name. His Truck racing expertise had certainly spread far and wide.

7-11 Signage

Back home in earlier years, I remember the signage on large banners within the car workshop. Walking into the workshop during the '60s before flashy electric signs existed, they were impressive.

They were hung very high up, thirty feet long and six feet deep. They were also twenty feet above the ground.

The sign read "Experience counts".

The second sign read "Satisfy the public".

Both signs got modified over a short period of time. The "O" in the first and the "L" in the second were covered.

It was a couple of months before the foreman saw the modification. Horrified, he demanded to know who did it.

Again, Mr Nobody was the chief culprit.

7-12 Number Plates

Number plates are issued to every vehicle in just about every country in the world. They are also used by Big Brother to identify vehicle mishaps and gain revenue. It also identifies the difference between identical production vehicles. Owners also have the option to purchase plates of preference.

This instance actually happened. I, as a manager, had the honour of having a company car. It was a perk, although the tax burden was another issue.

I had been driving it for about a year and booked it in for the annual service. Also, there was a small warranty repair to be carried out at the same time. I booked the car in and handed the keys over.

The service was in order but the warranty job was not. The vehicle was not registered. We checked the identification plate, and yes, it was not for this vehicle.

After much investigation, we found the correct registration was 198 and not the 199 on my plate. Fortunately, the second registration was also for a company vehicle. It was a different model but a demonstrator car, used by the sales team. A quick walk to the showroom made everything clear. A screwdriver fixed the problem. The front number plates had been fitted to the wrong vehicles.

Five minutes later, all was well. Matching number plates front and back, now the same on both vehicles.

Our vehicle preparation inspector (Grade One) was nicknamed Mullet. You can see why.

7-13 Second-Hand Cars

A directive issued to our sales team did not go down well. Any second-hand car that was traded in was to be made available to the staff. Understandably, a small handling charge should be added for the admin.

The sales manager was totally against this policy. He preferred to trade them to his buddy and, we guessed, get a buck. But the staff were meant to get the deal, and the sales team had to obey the rules. So, every possible restriction would be placed for purchasing such a vehicle—can't find the keys, can't find the salesman, can't find the paperwork. I did succeed in buying two cars eventually.

There was a limit, I believe, of only two per year and only for personal use. I did keep the first one for some time. It was a Red VW Golf Diesel.

I only sold this by accident. Well, because of an accident.

I was felling some chestnut trees behind my house when one took out the power line. This was early Sunday morning. We still had electricity, but half the street didn't. The tree had hit the overhead cable. It was now lying on the ground under the fallen tree.

The Electricity Board persons were on their way, and the engineer was a good guy and helpful.

The tree must have been blown down by last night's wind. An act of God. Not my chainsaw.

Thinking of Sunday callout charges, double time, engineer climbing the poles, new cable, the list could have gone on. The bacon sandwich worked. While the engineer was present, my wife was valeting her car. I was changing the glow plugs and checking the car's wellbeing.

After a further hour or so, all was well, and the neighbours had power again. The engineer said he was looking for a diesel VW for his wife.

"Look no further," I said.

The deal was done. We delivered it in the following days.

7-14 My XR3

I had two of these, absolutely loved driving them and survived lots of near misses. The first was a red one, the best. It got old and repairs started becoming expensive. With tears in my eyes, I sold it, and a newer black XR3 became my trusty vehicle. Never had quite the same spirit as the red one, but it was quick and reliable.

I then purchased a V6 newish Cortina Estate, a bargain, so the XR3 needed a new owner. I advertised it two or three times, but just wheel-kickers responded. Nobody had the money for this at the time. I was stuck with it.

A sales manager from a medium-sized garage lived locally to us. I knew him but not that well. My friend Neil phoned him and inquired about an XR3 they had for sale. The one they were selling was White, a colour he did not like. He wanted Black or Navy. That evening, George, the sales manager, bought my XR3 in black and paid in cash.

Neil could not get finance, so George now had a breeding pair on his forecourt.

7-15 Ford's Indian

This was not a new model that was to be unleashed but a rather unpleasant customer. It started OK, but the conversation then went cockeyed.

This customer said he worked for Ford's engine factory in Dagenham. Our Indian character needed a starter for his diesel Transit van. I collected this from our stock shelf and put it on the counter.

I explained to him that it was the only one we had that was reconditioned and in stock, and I quoted him the standard trade price of £88.00 plus V.A.T.

He then told me he was entitled to a forty percent discount off any Ford product. Explaining was difficult, but I was trying to tell him that this was not a Ford product. He was getting more and more irate by the minute.

Offering a similar product from the Ford Exchange scheme made it worse. Their price was almost £200.00. So, this discount card made the sale £30.00 more expensive than our unit. He just about flipped. Demanded to see the General Manager.

The Indian gentleman was now well up for the argument, with anger showing on his face. I explained my position to our Service Manager, who basically backed me up (surprisingly).

He did offer this gent a ten percent goodwill discount as a goodwill gesture. Stevo had been by the reception and covering this area while I had been away. Disappearing from the reception was Jim with the Transit starter he had just purchased. This was, of course, the only one we had.

I had a quiet chuckle. Stevo had seen the plot unfold.

Our customer could only buy the Ford unit now, albeit with the forty percent discount. Jim, of course, returned the unused starter the following day. We were happy to give him full credit.

7-16 Help Yourself

A wonderful gesture by the driver, who was a director of the Goldfellow drinks company. Their truck was doing poorly, misfiring and also almost undrivable.

It was booked in, and it was agreed that it should be completed within two days. Mr Goldfellow had told the receptionists and the technicians present to help themselves to the drinks in the truck.

Not a wise move, knowing the drinking capacity of most of those employed within our company. Tuesday was the first day for repairs to start. The job went well, heels were greased, injectors were serviced and ready to be refitted the next morning. The load on board seemed lighter though, but nobody was concerned.

The repairs were quickly completed. In came Mr Goldfellow to a truck with under half its original load. He was shocked. He sort of complained about the load being lighter than he thought.

It was agreed that a generous discount should be applied to their invoice. All was now balanced. The customer was happy and the technicians and receptionists well-watered. The job still made a profit, albeit at a slightly reduced amount.

The next episode in this tale took place a week or two before Christmas. The Goldfellow truck appeared again, this time with a small trailer. This was unhooked and parked in the orchard car park.

Entering the reception, Mr Goldfellow said he had brought us some seasonal joy. The truck had never been better, so again, please unload the trailer, and distribute the contents.

He was able to collect the empty trailer the very next morning. We had all signed a Christmas card, thanking him.

7-17 The Golden Arrow

Yes, courtesy of British Rail.

Our new building backed onto the railway line that ran from Maidstone to Ashford. One of the more expensive rail journeys was a trip on the famous Golden Arrow. British Rail's timekeeping is world-famous.

If you can see it, it has arrived.

Each Friday, at precisely 1.15 p.m., the Golden Arrow would pull to a stop just outside our rear doors. The precise timing was actually random. Anywhere between 12.45 and 1.45 p.m. was acceptable.

At just about 1.00 p.m., a heavy goods train was delivering its cargo forward towards the capital. It was generally over one hundred carriages long and took forever to pass by. Thus, the Golden Arrow was stationary for a few minutes or much longer. The kitchen got hot while the train was stationary, one of the waiters got overheated and regularly stood on the steps of the buffet carriage. He was a very well-spoken, coloured gentleman.

Many conversations followed over many weeks. He became part of the furniture. Our technicians were a class act, cunning, devious and always hungry. That said, they were very good at their jobs.

The well-dressed gentleman was named Charlie and, with his uniform, looked the part. The boys soon had Charlie dispensing half-pounders from the buffet carriage on a weekly basis.

These were not just burgers, they were British Rail Burgers, none of which were curly. Disaster arrived with the route change and the luxurious trip going direct to Dover. We never saw Charlie again but wished him well in his absence.

British Rail's burger turnover must surely have dropped, but profits must have been up. Hats off to Charlie.

7-18 Pigeon

These vermin have but one use—to annoy any technician while he does his work. From afar, they make a terrible din, one is bad, but a bunch can even haunt the dead. They seem to breed faster than rabbits to wind up more people for longer.

We had a health and safety issue with these creatures gaining access to our stores. Ours was an old building with the roof in poor condition, so entry for these seemed game on. There was manure everywhere. Very unhealthy. Something needed to be done. The local council was called to help assess the situation.

The six weeks between the call to the council and their operative's arrival was frustrating. A whole flock must have been waiting to arrive, we never saw the boat land. Our remedy was to pop a few off. Maybe the others would get the message and leave. No chance.

The deceased creatures were food for the fox that appeared nightly along the railway line. We were removing dozens each day, the fox brought his family along, and we were winning the battle.

Mr Jobsworth from the council said we were out of order doing what we were doing. He prided himself on being an accredited marksman and said the kills would be humane. The ones we killed were just dead. He also said the bodies had to be cremated so as to avoid disease.

The foxes did not go hungry, we just finished the job.

7-19 The Seagulls

It's not quite the same enemy as the previous one but well avoided.

We had noticed a buildup of branches and wood on the tall roof of our next-door workshop. Mummy seagull must have been working out with daddy seagull as family expansion was due.

The nest had been taking shape for three weeks and, by now, resembled a fortress. Their diet is battered fish, chips, sandwiches and ice cream along with a waffle cone if available.

Daddy appeared to have left his duties, so mummy was now in sole charge. She enjoyed our company, along with the generous supply of ready meals. Most of us had named her Gully in line with her ancestry.

Then along came Malcolm, straight from the egg, or hell in our case. It was about a month on when we first viewed Malcolm. He was already large and found pleasure in sitting on the roofs of parked cars. Gully had changed from her friendly fly-by, thanking us for dinner to an all-out attack. Malcolm was doing his deeds on car roofs, not just one roof, toilet duties shared.

He hopped from roof to roof with white donations equally spread. Gully was supervising this. Any human passing by was, of course, a challenge. Protecting her Malcolm was her sole aim.

We, too, had adapted. We carried dustbin lids and wooden hammers, and we started moving in groups of three or more for our own safety.

Many customers complained of potential injury when parking their cars. Something had to be done, so the local enforcement officer was called in. Nobody wanted the family injured (or worse), but he told us of his plan.

We thought, give the mother bird a speeding ticket and take her licence away. No. His plan was to cage them both and take them to the seaside town, a more natural home.

This was done and we assume they have a good life now in Hastings. We never did get a postcard from them.

7-20 Our Christmas Bonus

A time for thanks, giving and rewarding staff for loyal service.

The company had, for many a year, added a substantial something to the wage packets at Christmas. This was when we all got paid with real money by a senior manager or director. Their task was to deliver the wage packets to one and all each week. Just about half a week's wages were added and a small card, thanking people for their support.

This tradition went on for many years, but times changed things. In November, a notice went up that the annual Christmas gift was being halved. This was due to economic measures that were beyond the company's control. The disgruntled workforce spent many an hour discussing this policy. Morale took a big whack.

We still received a token gesture in our wage packets so, many were still grateful. Many years went by, and again, the Christmas cash gift was modified. It was now a Christmas Hamper, quite a large hamper, I guess, equal to the cash amount spent.

Again, not everyone was happy. Everybody got the same. The newly appointed apprentice got the same as a master technician. You could not please everybody. Anyway, who eats mature goat's cheese with a wax covering, usually in the motor trade? More like a block of medium cheddar with a slice of Hovis.

The original hamper baskets still hold favour and we still keep the tree decorations, reflecting better times.

Over the years, the hamper basket got smaller and smaller along with its contents. Eventually, the basket was replaced with a box. The whole tradition had gone up in smoke, many boxes remained on workbenches into January. This gesture was viewed poorly, but it showed signs of what was to come.

7-21 Our Christmas Draw

At its peak, we were a workforce of fourteen employees, all experienced and all characters. Always feeling obliged for their service, I tried to look after them and keep them happy. This effort was helped by our version of our Christmas package, the Christmas Draw.

Many regular customers appreciated good service and rewarded us with a donation. This could have been a twelve-pack of beer, maybe a couple of bottles of wine. One regular fruit farmer brought his van well-stocked not only with his fruit and veggies but also some imported items for us.

Everything was stored upstairs so as not to attract attention.

One customer offered us fourteen desk diaries, this was for replacing a drum of cleaning fluid that had leaked. Half of the annual displaced batteries had, over the past six months, been traded in for cash.

Our pot was getting bigger.

We spent some cash with Des The Egg. Fourteen dozen arrived the day before the share-out. The next week clock cards had numbers one to fourteen to denote which pile of goody became yours. Fourteen cardboard boxes were loaded full of Christmas fare, all just about balanced.

Barta, consumed by some as a whisky, was traded for two bottles of red. It was fun to watch. There was even an envelope with a couple of notes inside each. This had gone under the radar and lasted years until I took early retirement.

7-22 Air Tubes

These were all the rage in prehistoric times, a capsule could travel to a faraway destination in seconds.

A keyboard with preprogrammed destinations was essential. There were, in fact, two tubes, one a suck and one a puff. This relied on the ducting going around the departments to find its home and was controlled by compressed air.

If you sent some money in the tube and Accounts got it, that was a success. Always, paperwork was essential as one never knew the source of the capsule. Thus, many other items were mailed. Loose rice and sugar were among the other passengers.

The broken stink bomb caused havoc, but the source was revealed. It was traced back to the parts department by smell, and they had absolutely nothing to do with it. It arrived at the car sales manager's desk. He was not amused.

Various spiders did the rounds along with the jar of mustard that jammed the system. The lid was identified as faulty at dispatch. But from whom?

7-23 The Wasp Nest

Nasty little buggers without any known use. A whole heap of these little bugs racked up just outside our window. It looked like they knew when the window was open.

Their attack weapons were well-known, a sting with an evil poison to humans. In our defence, we had a secret weapon, we had paint spray.

As they entered, usually in formation through the open window, the spray was dispersed. We had tons of black, usually applied to remanufactured starters. Silver was also popular, this was used for spraying wheels and generally borrowed from the car valeting bay.

We also accumulated many of the more varied colours from a too-good-to-throw-away cupboard. The same fate greeted each and every wasp. A quick spray with the paint containing lacquer. This increase in body weight now gave Mr Wasp a problem. More revs were needed.

This was getting harder to achieve as their wings are mighty thin, so the slightest paint drop was an issue for them.

Eventually, gravity won, and the squadron was downed. A complete wipeout. But no. One had escaped and made its way into Worzel's room.

All we heard was, "The little shit has got me!"

We gave this wasp something special. He was the only one that whole day to be sprayed bright yellow.

Jacko was summoned to remove the nest, sprayed it with diesel, lit Swan Vesta, and all were gone.

7-24 Blackberries

It wasn't the mobile phone version but one of nature's free fruits if you can get near enough. The bramble growth at the rear of our unit was shared with British Rail. We had some corrosive and unhealthy chemicals that needed outside storage.

One particular acid-based drum was to be feared. It was obnoxious. Once this chemical had completed its useful life, it had to be returned to the manufacturer for disposal.

Our wash was also outside, so an abundant amount of water was available. We had a stainless-steel cabinet to contain this acid, with drainage back into the cabinet. Once drained and shaken to minimise any acid loss, it could be washed with high-pressure water.

Goggles and gloves were essential during this process. Most of the spray was directed at the brambles. They seemed to thrive on this.

Duffy thought he would pick some fruit and take it home for his Mum to make some jam. In about ten minutes, he had enough blackberries to fill an orange box. Mum was up for the challenge. She started by putting the fruit in a large, steel, blue-painted pot.

She added some sugar and heated it up. Apparently, the smell stunk the house out. The blue had come off the pot, and it gave out the acidic smell Duffy knew well.

This now cool, congealed mess was placed straight into the dustbin, pot and all.

7-25 The Italian Truck

We will call him Giovani. He drove all the way from Florence to the UK with a full load of furniture. The Artic unit was all that we had recovered, as the trailer was taken elsewhere for safekeeping. Once we checked, it was clear it was not going to be a quick fix.

The driving axle had literally blown up. There was more of the axle outside than inside. There were no signs of any oil, which probably assisted the failure. The whole axle and casing had damage. A new main housing and complete axle assembly were required.

Good fun and expensive. The Iveco truck was Italian-made, and the driver acknowledged the issue. His company authorised the repair, and the parts were ordered on a VOR basis—Vehicle Off Road.

Nothing was available in the UK. The parts had to come from Italy. They were ordered and were underway. Giovani was resourceful. He dined in our canteen and loved the bacon rolls.

He placed a standing order for two each day, his sleeper cab was his home with TV and music all day. Washing was not a problem, the Gents was free for him to use at any time. A new clothesline hung between the cab of the Artic and the downpipe from the canteen. All now know the colour, size and style of his underwear.

We did invite Giovani for a beer at Friday lunchtime. He accepted the invitation and consumed two large glasses of red wine. Italian of course. The second Friday, he again joined us with his truck on the mend.

Completed by 4 p.m., Giovani spent the last working hour, shaking hands with all the new friends he had made.

Chapter 8

Social Club

8-1 Car Rally

Car rallies and treasure hunts were a favourite. A lot of time and effort were spent by the organisers on a popular event.

A gathering of excited drivers waited for the Go sign. The question sheets were handed out. All the cars had a two-minute gap before they departed.

Mileage was taken and confirmed. 30 pubs were to be identified en route and their map references were given.

I knew 29, so we entered them on the answer sheet before setting off. My wife, our 9-year-old daughter and her classmate, a young friend, were both passengers and spotters.

We collected wool from a fence and a brick from a wall, which did not please the builder. Also needed was a bulb, so a bulb was unearthed from a lady's flowerpot. The egg that was required was purchased from the corner shop as it was chocolate and close to Easter. I did not fancy doing anything nasty to a chicken.

An antique shop held one clue. It was a pair of salt and pepper pots shaped like birds. They were one of the clues and were worth 10 points if we found them. Describe the salt and pepper pots, was the clue.

The correct answer was, of course, birds. They also allowed "Gone" as the answer. They were only £4 for the pair. We still have them now. Such a bargain and a clue that left the people who followed wondering what that clue was all about.

We were within a shout of winning a prize. The results were read out, and we had 29 correct pubs. The wrong one was the Snake and Stick located at the back of beyond. Never been by it, in it, or knew of its existence, but the map reference was spot on. We had found it, and my daughter was asked to write its name on the sheet as we drove slowly by.

I thought she had spelt it wrong. Maybe, maybe not.

She had written what she had seen on the door.

Public Bar.

Her penance was to wash the dishes for a whole week or walk the eight miles home alone!

8-2 Car Rally 2

It was a time trial and a set distance to follow with an ordinance survey map with sixteen clues.

With an estimated mileage of 27.4 miles and the time allowed—one hour and fifteen minutes—it should have been easy. Kim's car was recovered the next day after rolling off the Pilgrims' Way. Only his pride was hurt.

Oh yes, some body panels needed attention too—to go with the new roof.

At the top of Hollingbourne Hill, there is a square wooden signpost with four arms giving obscure local directions—Wormshill, The Warren, Newington and, I believe, Buttley Hollow.

We decided we needed to stop at this signpost to give some of our competitors a hand. Two of us lifted this heavy signpost out of its hole and turned it 90 degrees around. Bonzo took almost three hours and used just about a whole tank of fuel, covering almost 93 miles. He had got lost and arrived at the seaside.

He proved it by producing a stick of rock with "Leysdown" written on the candy. No one cared who won, only that the bar was open to celebrate someone's victory. Another well-supported event.

8-3 Football Team

The company had a fairly decent football team which was well-established in the local league.

As was customary, training was on Tuesday evenings with four pints of beer and three packets of Frazzles. This was after hacking a football around a field after a full day's work.

Saturday mornings were always a worry with hangover checks, near fatalities during working hours and so on.

Eleven players generally appeared, but one Saturday, all was not well. All eleven had turned up, changed into our kit, and the referee was present. The opponents looked challenging. A rugged bunch from Preston Hall. This was a local psychiatric hospital.

We were only playing the caretakers, but a whole bus full of inmates was here for a day out. They were marshalled exceptionally well, they all stood in a perfect line on the touchline. An eerie situation unfolded. Their support was not as expected. Nobody dared to move out of line. Some had turned around, some looked at their feet, some looked skywards, but nobody present was watching the sport unfold. Just about to start the match, but we had no football.

We were saved by some small lads having a kickabout with a size-four football. The regulation size is five which is about fifteen percent larger.

We negotiated a price and hired the ball for the duration of the match. We gave the boys fifty pence before the match and promised another fifty pence at full-time.

Our opponents were none the wiser about the smaller ball. To their credit, the supporters were taken in line back to their bus.

Nobody knew the score but the guy with the long coat saw an aeroplane.

8-4 In Nick

We were playing on some strange football pitches.

On one at Lenham, we had to chase the sheep off. One had a big crater at the side and at Hunton, there was a boggy pond behind the goal. Addington had a pitch on the side of a hill. Each was different but always a challenge.

We were asked to play a friendly match, a nine-a-side match, which was a first for me. I read the team sheet, and the venue was a total surprise. It was in Maidstone's prison. Never again have I visited, nor wanted to. We were given a tour of the sports facilities. Even at the time, it was second to none, certainly compared to my old school's physical education equipment. We changed into our kit and were ordered out in a single file.

The door was slammed shut and locked behind us. As always, we had on our bright yellow kit.

Intimidating wolf whistles made it unnerving. The whole of the prison's inmates must have attended, 400 or so of them. They were restricted to one side of the pitch. Our side had six substitutes and our linesman.

The kick-off was signalled by the referee blowing his whistle. The noise was intense. It sounded like four thousand or more people. They had two ex-professional footballers on their team.

They were banged up for accepting bribes. Today, their agents do it on their behalf. Soon, we were Three-Nil down. Jungler The Long, our striker, went on a run through their defence.

His shot to the goal was just a little high. It cleared the net, and then it cleared the forty-foot-high wall behind the goal.

To a man and well-orchestrated, the chant, "I'LL GO" echoed around the pitch from the forty thousand watching. Nobody actually went except a guy in a blue uniform.

8-5 Married Versus Singles

This match was vicious. Managers were advised not to play as they would be a target for revenge.

Things like breathing in a public place or reading the daily paper in printed order was a good reason for an attack.

It was an annual event that had repercussions as, generally, sick notes mounted the following week.

A few ringers were brought in by the married team, husbands of female employees. It was always a win for the singles, so a newer and more balanced version evolved.

8-6 Town Team Versus The New Depots

This levelled things up. The company soccer team had eight or so on each side. Also, in the company, were some very good football players who played at a higher level. All wanted to share in the challenge to be supreme champions for the year. Mote Park was the venue, and refreshments were laid out at the Bull on the Heath afterwards.

A proper referee was needed as it could get tasty. This, it did. The ball floated over, and I swear, watching the ball only, I hit the ball superbly well.

John Mayo, the opposing goalkeeper, had other ideas, bless him. It was him who I had kicked. He was out cold. It was truly an accident. These things happen.

His father-in-law, our regular left back, some sixteen stone of beef was running towards the collision. I was walking away after this coming together.

It wasn't his family member he was concerned about. He was heading for me. Well, I took off, and being younger and lighter than Winchie, I got away.

I was chased by this over-forty hooligan up to the children's swings, some three hundred yards away. Out of breath, both of us turned around. I followed him back to the match with a good distance between us.

No lasting damage to the goalie, but I kept well away from their left back. At the Ale House afterwards, all was well and forgiven, if not forgotten. Until next year.

8-7 5-A-Side Challenge

This was fought out at the local swimming baths, no, not in the water but a proper 5-a-side pitch.

We had about ten teams from all the expanding sections of our company. It was like a FIFA draw. Nobody knew how it was drawn, but nobody cared. There were three good teams, four just average.

Then there were the Accounts, three delicate young ladies between nine and five, the Accounts Manager and Bob, who talked good football knowledge, but could he play! He was brilliant!

The three assassins looked the part, they kicked everything that moved. If you stood still, you still got kicked. It was a struggle to try to play, but despite this, we had a few goals more.

We checked the numbers. They had started with six, they said their goalkeeper did not count. During the last few minutes, I think they had three additional players, the substitutes played on.

It was like the Alamo, a hoard of screaming women trying to kick you. A ball was deliberately left behind on the penalty spot. Our goalie, Neville, had already dived.

An open goal. Mini just about hit the corner flag. A good event again. Bob was seen hobbling around the following week, he had literally run himself into the ground.

8-8 The Football Final

We were not too bad at football, and one year, we got to the local league cup final. This was played at the Old Maidstone United Stadium, long since gone. After intensive training the week before the final in the Saxon Chief Pub, we had several plans underway.

Our Managing Director was getting excited and was due to attend. He had notices printed and displayed throughout our garage.

Lots of friends and family were coming along with a good few of the company workforce. On the day, we met as usual in the Saxon for a drink or two before heading to the stadium. We were not expected to win as the papermill team had 3000 employees to pick from. A very entertaining game, so fortunately, that day we managed the victory on penalties, after extra time.

My MD was ecstatic and had taken many action shots with his Brownie camera. Once developed, it looked like twenty-two matchsticks from two miles away. As a self-believing Royal, he carried little cash.

Wishing us well and to celebrate, he borrowed twenty quid from Charlie to buy two bottles of champagne.

Fortunately, the Local Kent Messenger had a photographer present. The MD had photos of all the action, 20 shots of people at 200 yards about half an inch high. Bless him.

8-9 Indoor Cricket

We used to play indoor cricket in the rear of the old bus depot at South Park. It was a five-a-side, we had seven players and rotated the squad.

We were, I believe, second in the mini-league, and due to play the third-placed team. The team we were playing was the local newspaper team.

None of the players actually worked there. It was a PR stunt that worked well. There was a well-known local football player from our town team.

In walked their star man. A certain Gary Mason, a heavyweight boxer and national champion. There was a beautiful pair of women, one on each arm, and a photographer from the local rag.

We started the match. It was my turn to bowl. I looked at Gary. He was massive. I bowled the first ball, and he missed it. The second ball was different.

A big swish, the ball just edging upwards from the bat.

It caught our Gary just under his hairline. He dropped to the ground, poleaxed. He was out of it, lying on the floor, and there was a lot of him.

The game had, obviously, stopped.

As I approached Gary, I could only think of saying, "Sorry."

An ambulance was called. Gary was now awake but wobbly on his feet. He was taken as a precaution but not kept in. The whole of the local paper's team followed him.

There was no mention of this in the next edition.

I think he was to go on and win a boxing champion's belt without hitting the deck again.

8-10 The Cricket Team

The team wasn't very good. Probably worse than that.

It was captained by Fullbier, the Company Secretary, Boring Billy, no mates. All the other local clubs liked playing against us. We were cannon fodder to them, but we always had a beer afterwards.

Our only good victory, I recall, was beating Hollingbourne on a Sunday Match. I don't know how. "Young Len" was our warranty clerk, looked 80 and wore specs to match.

The ball popped up to him slowly about halfway down the pitch. He juggled with it for three or four grasps, and there it was flat on the ground. Their batsman could do nothing but laugh, but as Len bent to retrieve the ball, he inadvertently kicked it.

It went a further few feet forward, still with a chance of a runout. Len kicked it again as he stood on his own fingers. Heaps of players were rolling about laughing.

Len was injured, so he was taken to the beer tent to recover. Barney's 11-year-old son substituted, so we were, then, a much stronger side.

8-11 Cricket at High Halstow

It was a proper team, which, for us, was a different league. We called in some guest players to make a team for the match.

Still, we never won, though it did not matter. Mr Ron bought all the beer, so the event was very well supported. I never knew why. Pitchers of beer until nobody remained standing helped. Mr Ron's cricketing was not as important as his ornithology, so his locals knew his needs well.

There was talk of the lesser spotted woodpecker being seen in Mrs Beal's field earlier. His newly painted Ford Capri was parked in MrsBeal's field. So, Mr Ron, with binoculars in hand, went to look for Woody.

On his return to the Capri, he found that the new paintwork was a mess. Mrs Beal's cows had taken a liking to the new paint taste. With their raspy tongues, they had taken the paint back to the primer. He was not happy. Having lost the match early, we were early in the pub.

What a shame, as Doug, our trusty driver, was downing his second pitcher. That would mean a long walk home. Shep came to the rescue. He had no driving licence but was a good driver in the garage.

Doug was now flat out across the back seat with five other passengers. Shep was now in charge, so the old Ford "Shed" headed for home. Shep did us proud with no Plods in sight.

We were delivered safely, all to our houses.

The Ford Shed was parked securely at the garage before 8 a.m. before the next day's work. Roll on next year's match!

8-12 Ghost Trip

An organised trip to the local town of West Malling was arranged with a guest speaker in tow.

This historic town dates back to the Roman conquest or before. According to the Ford tradition, we assembled in the pub on High Street and toured by foot. Appropriate clothing was necessary and a heavy fog was present.

The town's harrowing history began with a trip to the church graveyard. Our carwash character was in full funeral director's outfit, complete with a swinging hand-held lantern.

My wife showed her true identity—a long black coat, a witches' hat and a witches' brush broom. I did tell her there was no need to change from her everyday dress. So, that is what she wore.

In the churchyard, the scene was set. The fog was now a real pea souper. We were standing on the pit site where people who died in the

Great Plague were buried. Carmen, one of the highly strung Accounts ladies, was listening fully focused on the lecture being presented.

My thoughts went to the witch's broom. A slight tickle just above her high boots and just below her pleated skirt with the branches of the broom.

She thought that the hand of one of the sixteenth-century victims of the black death had grabbed her. The sound that came out of her was sharp, loud and in panic. Carmen ran 50 yards in three seconds flat.

The witch's broom was back in my wife's hand before another spell could begin.

8-13 The Ghost Trip Continues

An hour or so had gone by on the Ghost Tour, the trip was going well, and we were directed into an unlit passageway.

The passageway ran behind the restaurants and pubs on High Street. It was in the thick fog that was still ever present, and the undertaker, with his swinging lamp, starred.

He and my wife walked arm-in-arm towards the buildings.

Two young lady staff members were on the top stairs having a crafty cigarette. They saw the two creepy silhouettes approaching, screamed, chucked their cigarettes and dashed back into their workhouse.

For the second time that evening, the screams confirmed that this town was truly haunted.

8-14 Quiz Nights

It was another popular event and was very well-supported.

It was held in various watering holes in various parts of our town. The teams were made up of the staff with their partners and generally had a maximum of six people per team.

The Accounts department always wanted to be crowned the champions but rarely were. The Social Club secretary was a lovely lady and put a lot of time and effort into making this event swing.

The sheets were handed out, and a suitable name was selected. Number crunchers, Arthur Dalys Bangers, Dippy Diesels, Tuned Right Up and Anybody Need Servicing. These were just some of the titles selected for the teams.

The local landmarks proved to be a problem for most of our team as we never went shopping. We were better at identifying vehicle brand names, but famous people? Forget it. Nine of the ten answers we gave were Winston Churchill. Somebody did know the picture of the Queen.

I challenged it as it did not look a bit like Freddy Mercury. We now had two points, the Queen and very proudly, Winston was answer five.

I was expelled for a rush of blood that caused me to shout out the answer in the next round—General Knowledge, Question one: What is the most intelligent living creature next to man?

I knew the answer. Without hesitation, I blurted out—"Woman."

Men were falling about laughing, and women were booing. I was asked to leave for a cooling-off period, which was fine.

Our team was stronger without my help, and I was topping up the beer on our table anyway. As expected, we came last, and we won the Best Answer of the Evening prize. We won the crème egg.

The question that got us the prize—How many days in a leap year?

We answered, "Only seven—Monday, Tuesday, Wednesday, Thursday, Friday, Saturday and Sunday."

Were we wrong?

8-15 London Shows

We went on many of the capital's best shows over many years.

The Social Club used to subsidise the costs of these visits and organise the coach transport. It also meant that everybody gathered at base camp, so in theory, all were present and accounted for.

At least we were all present before the trip.

The downside of this was it took forever to get to the centre of London. The advantage was, of course, that we were dropped just outside the venue. Parking, therefore, was not an issue, neither was trying to find the theatre.

Once the show is over, things should be equally well-organized—52 people returning to the bus. Only 38 made it safely back. That left 14 people walking the streets as they had come out of the wrong exit.

It was directly on the opposite side of the theatre from where we had entered. The "Turn Right on Exit" instruction should have been reversed for this particular exit. The search party did retrieve the stragglers, who were rounded up, captured and held in custody.

The trusty bus was summoned to collect the now shivering, famed fourteen people. The bus arrived, and we had the usual banter—it was always the same people who were the last ones back.

8-16 Gliding

It was the middle of summer and for once, a bright, sunny day.

All of us made our way just short of Dover, a small village, at the top of the cliffs. There was a cricket ground sharing its social facilities with the gliding club. Our social club had negotiated a day out with glider rides, and friends were invited to boost numbers.

This was an ideal spot as the heat from the sea and the Dover port rose up the white cliffs. The first flight took off, and one of our brave staff made his will before departing. He came back alive, and with full-on excitement, persuaded many others that it was OK. The procession went on from ten in the morning until early afternoon with loads of flights. Pauline, one of my guests, was unsure of taking part, but the best of a pint of gin was what tipped the balance.

She walked to the glider confidently. Her very high heels and miniskirt were a sight to behold. Then, with the climb into the glider, the miniskirt hitched up, underwear now on display, and a cheer now went up.

It was rumoured that during the ten-minute flight, Pauline never opened her eyes. Also, it is unclear if Pauline did manage to get into the five-mile-high club. The craft landed safely with a bump. Pauline had to dismount. All eyes were on this spectacle.

After a generous amount of applause, Pauline's long legs wobbled to the social hut. A large gin and tonic were her reward.

Her husband asked if she had enjoyed the flight.

Her reply was, "I was scared shitless."

There was no chance of an encore for the hungry watching crowd. However, the day was a resounding success as everybody who wanted to fly did.

8-17 Ten-Pin Bowling

This was yet another well-supported event, and we often had eight lanes booked for the evening.

There was always a prize on offer for the best score of the night. So, the same old faces used to fight it out, two from the showroom and one from Accounts. These were regular team players, not just the turn-up-and-bowl kind.

The burgers and chips that were on offer made it a bigger challenge. Somehow, you just knew that your turn was due when the oil from the chips was on your fingers.

There were people dropping the ball. I remember our Neville launching one backwards. His strike was successful, three half-pints of beer and a glass of water.

My wife had a night to remember, hit an eight and two more with the spare. She followed this with five consecutive strikes. She was on for a big one.

A couple from the management team were impressed and came and watched discreetly. Her peak had passed, but her score of 234 that night was our Social Club's best ever. It took her some weeks to come down from that impressive achievement.

8-18 Coach Trip to See the Christmas Lights

It was a very well-supported outing to see the Christmas lights with two coaches carrying approximately 50 people each.

July was probably not the best month for this, but we made the best of the opportunity. We loaded the coaches on Square Hill Road and proceeded to Detling Hill. An urgent stop for most male travellers was for the first loo break.

The 60-minute journey was well into its second hour after the fifth stop for natural calls. Margate was in sight. We dismounted and entered the approach road to Dreamland—the most famous watering hole was an unplanned destination.

Fortunately, I guess 80 percent of our group found this same venue by accident. Live music, beer flowing, and the noise was getting louder.

Flint was a dab hand at playing the spoons. Wint could play the bones. Flint & Wint, two brothers who entertained us all, had a guest with them. A certain clever Trevor.

This Trevor was at the same secondary school as me. His claim to fame was drinking the ink from the inkwell. He had a blue tongue before any outbreak was known in the farming industry.

Being the worse for wear, Big Trevor stood up. He walked straight up to the drummer in the band.

Suddenly all went quiet. Scrap on? No.

Trevor picked up a drumstick and gave the base drum one big bang. The drumstick was then returned to the drummer, and Trevor returned to his seat to cheers and applause. The show went on.

Many were sick, some slept, some attempted Dreamland. All were accounted for. Not a single Christmas light was seen. Not even in July.

The return trip was notorious for the two unicorn trophies in the first coach. One blue and one pink. It appeared that they were trying to prevent their extinction.

The display, of course, was in full view in the rear window of the coach.

8-19 Dog Racing

Both Catford and Crayford were the two tracks we supported.

One or two coaches were hired, depending on the uptake. There were 13 races during the evening, it was a good time to relax, and the £2 stake money on each race was nearly always wasted. Sometimes, we get a winner, which means we should break even. Two wins, and the beer was also paid for. Three wins, and we did not have to work Monday.

We had only one coach on the Saturday in question, and we were off to Catford. The driver was an odd character, we had been with him before. As we arrived at Crayford, we told him the error of his ways.

We explained we were nine miles away.

Fortunately, Polly's partner was a London Courier driver on board and knew the route to Catford. A hurried rush was on, and we disembarked right outside the front entrance.

The people who had booked a meal deal rushed to be seated. They played catchup with the rest of the punters. The rest of us just started at race five out of thirteen.

8-20 Trip to Poole in Dorset

This was a more serene trip than the Margate lights, dog racing or the London shows, which were short-haul trips.

Meeting in the British Queen, a pub long since past, we had a good fill. Again, the first stop from Square Hill was Brenchley Gardens, some two miles from kick-off. Needs must be met.

We stopped again at Clacket Lane Services, a further half-hour on. And then again well before Poole, which was our planned destination. Fortunately, our driver was OK.

He loaned me a marker pen, so I could add my touch to the route display board. On the reverse side of buses '62 to London Board, his regular route, I added our itinerary Fords to Poole—The Incontinent Tour. Please bring your own toilet roll.

The trip was voted a success by most of the ladies, partners and wives. They all spent well.

In Poole was a porcelain manufacturer of specialised pottery. Not knowing what to expect, I was surprised. I had an early vision of a sort of caveman in a loincloth, making the jugs that you see on the walls of caves.

This was an up-to-date factory, mass-producing tableware for households across the land. It seemed that every lady from our party purchased a dinner set. Surprisingly, they all had different names. I now call my regular dinner plate Terry. I think it's trendy.

The company we visited could now afford to build a new wing to their sales area from the profit of our trip. The thought crossed my mind on the return trip home.

Did we all really need new plates? Ours now live in a distant cupboard but are available should royalty visit.

8-21 First International Trip

We were branching out, cashing in on the booze cruise adventures. A full coach with the usual stops to Dover, passports in hand, and we were on. The limit was a maximum of four boxes of beer per person. The 50 seated punters had, therefore, purchased 200 boxes.

Doug, the coach operator, was a lovely character, and we frequently repaired his chariots. Most of the chariots were single-deckers discarded by London Transport once they covered two million miles.

Straight to Eastenders', well before City of Europe was born. Our investment was complete, bottles were chinked, and the first hundred cases went onboard. The other side opened, ready for loading.

An almighty crash occurred. Most of the 100 crates were now under the coach. The very mature wooden floor of the underside storage was also on the ground, mostly below the crates.

We unpacked the floor and salvaged most of the bottles. Hardly any were broken. Resourceful as ever, we commandeered a few pallets that were stacked nearby. Doug now had a new solid floor on his bus in the storage section.

But wise to this, we unpacked the second side, reinforcing this floor before the same event occurred.

We did not even charge him for the repairs or the destruction of his coach, as he called it. All wine bottles were to be carried inside and put safely on or under the seats. We made it all the way back but resembled the noise of a local milk float for the whole journey.

There was some mention at the customs checkpoint. Cheeky chappie that he was, he suggested that our vehicle should be registered as a tanker, not a coach.

8-22 Trip To Paris

Disney World was booked, and off we went. We got there on time and went for the first pint of the weekend.

We checked into our hotel, which was eight stops outside Paris, and accessible by SNCF for just six Euros. We had our daughter with us for her twenty-first birthday surprise present.

The coach took us to and from Disney, so no hassle there. The plan was, hotel, shower and back to Paris for an evening meal with drinks aplenty.

The meal went well, drinks went better, but the pissoirs were not to be found. A privet hedge, which appeared to be dehydrated, was engaged for interim relief. Now, to the train station. All 16 of our group were on the train. Two stops on, the noise was getting louder.

As we stopped, all 30 thousand fans from Paris Saint-Germain seemed to get into our carriage. Upset by this, mainly as they had no tickets but had more alcohol than us, we stood amongst the mob.

One handed me a bottle of strong beer, which I downed as if it were my first. A great cheer went up and the ice was broken—no fighting but glasses thrown from the open windows to celebrate.

Still cautious about this situation, we got off the train but were two stops short of our hotel. The women in our party were looking for the toilet, and most of us men needed a second opportunity.

A rose garden with water features was en route, with a construction area fenced off for security reasons. The women disappeared to all corners of this site for natural calls.

My wife asked me to guard the passage entrance to a new housing block. She was relieved to find relief. My guard duty was not perfect. The security guard approached.

My wife was in full flow as the Alsatian, along with the guard, turned the corner.

"Bonjour," I said as I disappeared.

Both the guard dog and the security guard did not speak English and departed.

My ears were boxed until we got back to the crowd for the two-mile trek to the hotel. My salvation was to find a wrapped, red rose on the fountain dumped by a no-show for a date.

I presented this in front of our crowd and was duly rewarded. We got back, and the bar was shut.

Merde!

8-23 24 Hours of Le Mans

It was another event organised by our social club. It turned out to be an all-male outing. One of our salesmen, who had a PSV licence, agreed to drive the coach, which helped keep the cost down.

In line with the company's unwritten law, the bus did have some refreshments stored underneath. The three-day jolly boys' outing was up and running. Packing was limited. Underpants and T-shirts were essential, so were our passports.

On the ferry, only four of the troupe were sick. They must have been seasick. Lager could not have been responsible as everybody drank lager, and only four were sick. We mounted the chariot and were reminded by the issues at the first interchange that we were in France.

By the time we were on the correct side of the road and collected our luggage that was now scattered across the floor of the coach, we were well on our way. We all had a sleep on the coach, I think, including Tony, the driver.

At Le Mans, you could smell the atmosphere. The vehicle fumes from 200,000 petrol engines were thick in the air. The race had started by the time we parked and trudged the five kilometres or three miles, whichever came first.

We had a good position to watch the race, just after a corner, so, for a couple of hours, we watched in awe. Never seen so many quick headlamps. Went back to the coach for some more sleep. Were cold, wet, bored and with ears suffering burnout.

Never returned to the procession for further punishment. The race was over. Yippee!

People returned en masse from the spectacle. It had been a full house. The car park was jammed. The excitement to escape was chaotic although Tony held his own. He repelled many a French car as they were wary of a right-hand drive coach, blowing its horn.

The 50 or so passengers, waving their fists aided his cause.

We had 18 hours before boarding the ferry, so a trip was voted on, so off to Paris we went. Entering the Paris ring road was a challenge and, of course, we went off at the wrong exit. So, a lengthy conversation about driving down the fold line on the map took place.

We found a coach stop just outside Paris at the Fleur de Lys public house. This was a mixture of a pub, a restaurant and a night club with music and much action. The bus was rested, and we were fed and watered using French opening hours. There aren't any.

Back on the bus again—four hours of sleep, and the same four sick again after the boat ride. Home, finally back to base, and the crowd dispersed. Shower, change and out for a beer. What a good trip!

8-24 The Christmas Social

Every year, the company had a gathering at one of the local hotels.

The organisers put hours of work into this event. A special thanks should be recorded for these folks. The first few years the party took place at The Tudor House. It had character and suited us well.

As a first-year apprentice, I did not know what to expect when the band announced the Ford choir was to sing.

Everybody was gathered around the bodyshop's manager who was a proper pianist unbeknown to me. He rattled off six or seven carols, and the newly formed male choir actually knew the words. It was wonderful.

As the hymns went on, gradually the band joined in. I felt this was the true spirit of Christmas.

This venue was ideal for our needs, we were sorry to learn a few years later that a fire burnt it to the ground.

Forced to relocate, the Star Hotel in the centre of the town was next in line. The atmosphere was not the same as before, but a good time was had by all.

The company was getting larger, purchasing depots around the county and beyond. With the Star now closing, the only location local to us was Greenways. For a few years, this had been home for our Christmas venue.

All social club members had an invite with a partner. Tickets were twenty-five pounds on the black market.

The next venue was the Great Danes. Again, quite a plush hotel with three dance halls. This was to be our home at Christmas for many a year.

I recall the raffle prizes were well worth the investment, a large colour TV being a major prize. There were about forty prizes in total, so there was a good chance of winning one. Not the TV but won the cutlery set. Cheers went up, and then my wife won some bed linen. Time went on, some prizes were still on offer, and we had another win.

"Shake it up," and similar comments were heard.

My wife disastrously chose a basket of smellies from the Bodyshop in town. Our table was not too far from the MD's, and his wife who was presenting the prizes, handed this over.

"You can't drink that," I called out.

Many chuckled.

Towards the end of the draw, our number came out again.

My wife said to the astonished MD's wife, "I have strict instructions this time to choose a bottle." Again, my wife said calmly that she didn't drink.

The MD's wife said, "But I know a man who does."

On another occasion, my wife was unwell, actually bedridden, and it was the night of the social. Panic set in as it was always one of the best days of the year.

At my wife's suggestion, I decided to take a stand-in. I guess by now I was in my late forties. So, with a phone call to my uncle's daughter and consent from my uncle, it worked well. Mel was a twenty-year-old and collected me at seven p.m. in her car. She looked fabulous. It was game on.

On arrival in the foyer, drinks were taken, and everybody shared pleasantries. None of my staff knew that my wife was ill and was unable to attend.

Nobody wanted to talk to me. They avoided any embarrassing conversation.

For people brave enough to enquire who the young lady was, "This is my mum," was my answer, stumping the conversation stone dead.

Mel was made for the part. She must have been embarrassed but took it all in her stride. Once seated, I had the good grace to explain the situation. "My mum" was suitably welcomed.

Chapter 9
Technical College

9-1 Further Learning

Day release with pay was like school with a wage. Something new and not to be wasted. I was warned by Butch, who was a senior apprentice, of a certain Mr Wilson. He was a strict and opinionated old-school teacher.

Tug, as Mr Wilson was known, was, therefore, already an enemy. The Ford garage and Mr Wilson were arch-rivals.

Like a Derby football match, someone had to lose.

He called out my name, "Sam from Ford's."

"Yes, Sir," I said quite loudly and standing tall.

"We don't like Ford's people here," was his response.

"You are Mr Wilson," I replied. "We, at Ford's don't like you either."

From then on, we both had mutual respect. At least on the surface.

9-2 The Bounce

Learning the motor trade skills was a challenge. Physical study was a subject deemed essential.

Our teacher for this challenge was Mr Rust. He was a poor entrant from the UK fencing team of 1952. The thing I noticed was that a Viking could slay him with one blow.

PE kit of shorts and singlet was a challenge, and I often forgot or dismissed it as unnecessary. The particular day in question involved almost everyone in our class—20 or so mortals. Mr Rust initially refused our request for sword fighting with tipped sabres, which he proudly had on display.

The trampoline was already in position, so it seemed perfect for entertainment. Twenty or so vehicle technicians simultaneously mounted this bouncy castle in various dress styles.

My jeans were held securely with my studded "ROCK RULES" belt as no shorts were available. At the bottom of the sack of technicians was Slim Wiggie, a poor soul who only had shorts and trainers but no shirt or vest on. On top of Wiggie was me with my belt across his chest.

Not too much of a problem, but for the balance of convicts, attempting to move on top of us both. The whistle blew, the bodies unravelled slowly and dismounted the sack of the trampoline.

Just two were left. I climbed out, which left just Wiggie. Motionless. He was breathing but was branded ROCK RULES across his chest.

No lasting damage occurred, and he's still a good mate today.

9-3 General Studies

General studies were always a problem as it had absolutely nothing to do with the motor trade. I am sure our left-wing teacher was employed to fill the space as nobody else was available.

He also failed an advanced course of rubber band counting and tasting. One afternoon, he decided to play a 33 record of some Indian mystic culture and left us to appreciate its benefits.

The sitar was not an instrument I recall being in the top 20, so it was somewhat wasted on us in the motor trade. We added to the culture just a little by upping the volume, restarting the disc and carrying out other minor adjustments.

Some 15 minutes later, he returned to find the same 20 technicians, jiving to the '78 version of the same vinyl record. The result was double speed plus a bit more. The noise resembled something from The Goon Show.

He came in, uttered oaths and took home his record player. He was not seen again by our class. Success!

9-4 Tyre Change

Most cars in the '60s had tyres with tubes that were becoming more reliable.

Nails and screws were the worst enemies, as they are today, but repairs were then cost-effective. There was no such thing as a worn tyre, and a replacement was due only when the metal core was visible. One of our musts was knowing how to change a tyre.

Since my apprentice days, specialists have sprung up everywhere to do just this. Our instructor was at it again, and our training tyre must have been changed forty thousand times. It was loose on the rim and just about fell off.

However, we had a student who had a puncture, and the spare was on the vehicle. This now was a real job. A real puncture. The wheel and tyre were mounted on a jig. This was essential as chasing a wobbly wheel around the workshop is not easy.

The jig is waist-high with a centre-threaded spindle and a tapered wing nut to hold the wheel centrally. The tyre pressure must be released. If it is flat, it saves a job.

Slowly spin the wheel by hand, checking for impact damage or more likely, damage by nails. Marking a fault with a crayon is advisable because water will not wash it off.

Today, there are units that rotate the wheel while the tyre is being removed by an inbuilt lever. We did not have this in the dark ages. We had two tyre levers. The tyre bead, when in use, sticks the tyre to the rim.

Once the pressure is released, there is nothing to keep this bead in place. A good wallop with a rubber hammer and it's free but inside the wheel rim. Tyre lever one is put in position between the rim and tyre.

Tyre lever two is put in beside the first one, loosening the tyre from the rim. Gently the tyre levers move the tyre bead over the rim, continually moving one lever around the rim.

Eventually, the bead is more outside the rim, and then it pops over the rim. Using the same process, the remaining bead should be easier to remove. The danger points of this job used to be shifting the first bead.

The first lever is under the bead. Care must be taken while the second lever is pushed inside the bead and pressure is applied to the lever. If the lever slips, this missile (lever two) is off, heading for anything in any direction. This is probably one of the most necessary advances in engineering within the motor trade.

The jig now rotates the wheel automatically. No levers but fixed dollies that do all of the work safely.

9-5 Lead Wings

Tuition for the students was always subject to keeping them interested during the training. So, what better way than learning a procedure on one's own car.

This was my very first car, a Ford Prefect, purchased for £37 from a neighbour. As with most cars of that era, rust appeared almost by order. We believed manufacturers built this in on the production line.

Mine had a matching pair of rusty wings, as did most Ford Prefects. The instructor at the college advised me on how to fix this, using lead sticks and flowing this in.

Firstly, I gave the wing a good beating. The rusty patch, the size of a matchbox, had trebled in size. My instructor showed me how to flux the remaining good parts of the wing and then apply the lead.

I was getting on quite well, working towards a proud conclusion when, suddenly, my progress halted. The idea, he said, was to gradually apply the lead and build up a thin layer and then another layer. He was a natural, making the job look so easy. I acknowledged his advice and thanked him.

Once he moved on, I continued and, eventually, the wing looked good, needing just a touch of paint.

Next week, I was excited about the other wing. I had whacked it, yes, and a lot more attention was needed, but we could not continue that day. New lead sticks were due to arrive the following week. My instructor apologised for the delay and said that we had fourteen sticks on Monday when he checked them.

They had only two remaining. The other twelve were on my wing. For that weight, there was no need to lower the suspension. He assisted me the following week and proved the wing could be fixed using a maximum of three sticks.

Oh dear! I never wanted to be in a body repair shop anyway.

9-6 The Forge

Metal work was a side issue with us but essential for a blacksmith.

The forge was fired up, bellows were in place for enhancing the heat and all ready for horseshoes. I had never seen a horseshoe on a Cortina but lived in hope.

Forging was taught and locked in my memory bank should any vehicle suffer a flat horseshoe. But all was not wasted. Once it was up to temperature, the forge had other uses. The sandwiches in our packed lunches were introduced and lightly toasted. A culinary delight until one fell into the fire pit, caught fire and set off the smoke alarm. Quite an outcome as the assembly point, which was the evacuation area for the whole college, was outside.

The girls from the front building were evacuated, as the alarm was for the whole college. Hair do's and make-up running down their faces along with a wet T-shirt competition. Wiggie was the centre of attraction but without his lunch.

9-7 The Shared Canteen

The whole college came together for meals. It was our chance to meet young ladies and try to impress them.

The challenge was on. The orange drinks dispenser was located at the end of the food area. Plastic cups were in a carrier beside this automated contraption. The objective was to take the cup, and the next drops down for the next victim. A sixpence coin was inserted in a slide that operated the orange juice ration. We helped by sticking a sharpened piece of welding rod through the bottom of the next bunch of cups.

This rod resembled a knitting needle jammed into the stack of cups in the dispenser. Once the rod was removed, havoc reigned.

Quite an event as most of the drinks had run out of the victim's cup before they reached their tables. That day, many students appeared to have incontinence issues many years before its time.

9-8 Smoking

Smoking, a vile habit, was allowed in the canteen, so there was another exercise of entertainment.

The ashtrays had four cutaways for placing the cigarettes. Four lit cigarettes were perched here. The salt and pepper on each table were the ammunition for this exercise. A very liberal helping of both was added to the smouldering cigarettes. Smoke started rising in a short time. The air turned rancid. It resembled mustard gas from a military encounter.

The fog grew in the canteen, and we were gone. This was the sport for the day. Many of the young ladies left with streaming eyes. Mission accomplished.

9-9 The Megger

One of the many advanced tools we were introduced to was the megger. Wind the handle, and an electrical charge was generated and stored inside this unit. We were read the riot act for this, but it was known not to carry a fatal charge. The workshop was prepared.

There were no seats in the workshop, so we all sat on the workbench. A sturdy, industrial, solid wooden bench with an angle iron circling the wood for protection against damage.

All were gathered, and we were being taught by Sid, our workshop teacher. To the man, everybody jumped in unison, shouting and hollering.

The megger was accidentally discharged, and both the leads were attached to the metal edge of the bench. This action did prove instructive, as pushing the button confirms the instant release of the charge.

Some 80 volts were instantly shared by all through the metal bench frame and into the arse area of all presently seated.

This could not happen again as the megger was locked away for health and safety reasons.

9-10 The Automatic Gearbox

The other notable memory is of stripping down an automatic gearbox. This unit could almost take itself apart as it had been apart so many times before. No oil inside, so once stripped, everything was already clean. Not like the real world, covered in oil, grime and dirt.

Our specialist repair workshop unit was on the fourth floor, which housed these vehicle sub-assemblies. On a hot July summer day, the need to open the windows of this greenhouse was obvious.

My gearbox was rebuilt for the 344th time in its life and on completion, Mr Ballcock checked our work. He was pleased as all went well, nothing visibly left over and all checks passed with top marks.

Before this appraisal, four of the sixteen ball bearings that appeared to be spare were relocated out through the window.

I did not want to strip the gearbox down again. I had the knowledge of how it worked. Fortunately, the ball bearing's fall from the elevated position was interrupted. Tug Wilson's Volkswagen Beetle assisted in arresting the bearings' fatal fall with its roof being the target.

He should not have parked it there, as the roof of the Beetle will testify. The four trophy dents were testament.

9-11 Lunchtime

Officially, we had one hour for lunch. Excellent in summer but maybe too long in the winter months.

I recall two incidents, but I am sure there were more. Midsummer had arrived, and it was a super-hot day. What could be better than a trip up the river!

We hired four boats. Wiggie, Elbow, Stephen Fry (no, not that one) and me. These had a mower-size engine onboard and reached a top speed of five miles per hour. Two shillings and sixpence deposit and a shilling per hour.

We paid in full and with our hard-earned coins. We were on a mission. To Malta. No, not the island but the watering hole on the river.

Arriving at our destination, we ordered four pints and gulped them quickly. The return trip was downhill, no I mean downstream. So, the aim was to get back within the hour.

We were well in time as we approached the high-level bridge, just a little further to go. We passed the first town bridge on the river bend. Disaster struck then. Wiggie was on the inside track, leading by almost a length. I saw an opportunity to gain some ground.

Again, to correct myself, some river.

I reached over and pulled the plug lead off of his engine's spark plug. The boat slowed, and I got the full voltage from the plug lead. I jerked back and quickly released the lead. Both of us watched the lead disappear into the murky Medway.

The other two sailors came across, and we calculated that the three should return quickly to the jetty. This we did and got our half-crowns back.

Wiggie walked back along the towpath and joined us on the bridge. His half-crown was forfeited but it was worth it.

The now scuttled boat with the engine submerged came bobbing along well past the jetty. It had just the nose or bow sticking out of the water. The chap who hired us these boats was more interested in salvaging his boat than chasing us down.

From that day on, we never went near that jetty.

9-12 Lunchtime Meals

What could be healthy with fish and chips but not from the Medway. We had an excellent restaurant in town. The Seven Seas, it was always painted blue.

Many students used to dine there because it was genuinely very good. And cheap. Each of us sat down at the same table after placing our order, all paying separately. We were sitting there, behaving ourselves, when there was a commotion at the counter. Somebody had ordered a bag of chips to go and added salt but did not expect to pour as much as she did.

The top of the large salt pot somehow fell into the chips along with most of its contents. After it was cleared up, a fresh helping of fried spuds was provided, and all was then well. Wiggie had undone the top of the salt pot. Not nice.

Eventually, our dinners arrived, even the waitress service was at no extra cost. I checked the salt pot before taking a fair covering. We were at ease and feeding well. Wiggie thought ketchup would add to the flavour of his large cod.

He picked up the bottle and gave it a fair shake. The sight of blood was everywhere. Again, the top came off. As well as the four of us getting covered, the ceiling had a liberal pasting. Wiggie now had a red fish that matched his shirt.

We were expecting to be escorted from the premises, but the manager came and apologised. He refunded us for the four meals and gave us a note to come back again, on the house.

Who loosened the ketchup lid? It was me.

Chapter 10
Repairs of a Different Kind

10-1 My Manager

He was Chief Petty Officer "Dumpty", as we called him. He was a character, an engineer from the war, and experiences that he delighted in recalling.

He was resourceful and if stuck, would be a man you would want on your side. It was said that if you were stuck in the desert, he would be the man to get you home. He would cough, cough again until he was hoarse. He would then ride the horse home.

When repairing anything, he would do it his way—always using the minimum number of the necessary parts.

Most things worked, but sometimes they fell short, as parts that needed replacing were deemed still serviceable.

This man was brilliant if you judged his correct actions and separated the unwise shortcuts that were ever-present.

10-2 The Fuse

In the early part of my reign and before I moved from passenger car repairs, there was a move afoot that interested me.

The company was to open a small fuel injection shop. I needed experience for my National Craftsman Examination. Diesel-powered vehicles in trucks and tractors were now commonplace. In an economical move, the specified area for this new diesel workshop was under the canteen stairs.

The truck vehicle technician was formerly kicked out. Electricity supply was, of course, not built for all the power needed for a diesel workshop which had a fair amount of specialist equipment. There was no three-phase supply.

A compromise was reached and a three-phase supply would be professionally installed. After a management meeting, Dumpty, the manager, would proudly install and improve it himself. The 240-volt Dumpty electricity system would become famous.

Three large wooden benches were now in place around the walls with four wall sockets for each bench. The secondhand test bench took pride of place. It looked new, the three-phase was connected and ready to rumble.

Connecting the 240-volt supply to the wall sockets was the next project. This involved running rubber-coated cables under the linoleum flooring for many small machines and power tools.

There were probably 24 cables with some crossing one another. The linoleum resembled a wave pattern where the cables lay.

All good to start with, but after a "short" time (excuse the pun) the fuse blew. The floor was marked with a cross to mark danger. That was where we did not walk and a larger fuse was fitted. As more current was needed, now the fuses blew more often.

A second cross was added to the linoleum as it was not a safe place to walk. Then a third. Now the floor had many crosses and, of course, we added some noughts where we could walk. The fuse box was constantly singing or humming, all the fuses used had grown in size. So, now a nail was used instead of the fuse, which solved the problems. All was well, as we went about our duties playing hopscotch with the crosses and the noughts.

The nail even glowed when the lights were off. The General Manager saw this still glowing after hours.

He immediately called in professional sparkies who could not believe what they witnessed.

10-3 Watch and Clock Repairs

Repairing watches and clocks was Dumpty's hobby and a source of income. It was evident from the outset that he was not a natural but was always willing to do his best. Around his office were various time-keeping units that were being calibrated after a repair.

Delicately removing the back to access the working components was easy. The service usually involved washing their insides with our injector cleaning fluid. My self-appointed duty was to wait until he was called away for a period of time. I could then give them all a tweak.

Push some forward by a couple of minutes, some by five minutes, some just needed to be pulled back in time.

By the next hour, the times were all over the place. My help was only part of the problem. Ian, being an equally willing little helper and unbeknown to me, was doing exactly the same to the clocks. Five minutes added here and there to my adjustments made the clocks' times random at best.

Dumpty would reset them all again after lunch and a further calibration was applied. This was again subject to both Ian's and my interventions with further ongoing adjustments. After a number of days, he got them to the best position and let the owner advise him of the necessary calibration.

That was if they ever worked again.

10-4 Alternators

This was a necessary improvement to the dynamo for vehicles with new-fangled electricals.

At the outset, replacing this mysterious component was the only option. This was a challenge.

Stripping these down was a mechanical issue, which we were partly capable of doing. Gradually, we could test all the internal components, and parts were becoming available. Testing these alternators was not always easy as some were of very different shapes. Clearly, wires needed to be attached and a battery connected to the test leads and the alternator rotated.

Dumpty was testing a newish unit from a commercial vehicle. It had no provision for bolts but sat in a cradle on the vehicle, but this was no deterrent. A tobacco tin was used on the top and the bottom, and the alternator was "secured" to the fuel pump test bench.

The nut holding the pulley had a suitable socket used to drive the alternator. It wobbled as it started to turn. All was out of alignment with impending disaster as it rotated. More speed—more wobble.

Wurzel had discreetly blown up a polythene bag like a balloon with compressed air until it burst. A very loud bang was heard, Dumpty was clearly shocked and jumped a good foot in the air.

Wurzel legged it and was being chased by Dumpty with a two-pound hammer threatening death.

10-5 Snuff

No, Dumpty had not died of fright but enjoyed this bygone habit of clearing one's nostrils.

Each morning, at approximately 8.30, he would sniff this mixture from his silver tin. I would give him 10 minutes as he sniffed, sneezed and coughed—was it doing some good? Ian being as helpful as ever decided to uprate the snuff contents.

Most of the snuff was removed from the tin at a suitable time. Black pepper was a fair exchange. We waited for the clock to tick around. All the staff were out of sight as Dumpty's surprise began.

There was a sniff, a sneeze, then a holler of abuse and an empty workshop. It was fair to say that by lunchtime, his red eyes had stopped running, but there was no lasting damage.

10-6 Turbochargers

The turbocharger is a something-for-nothing device that uses exhaust gas to spin a rotor. The shaft has another rotor on its other end, which pushes air into the engine when it's spinning.

This basic principle, therefore, uses exhaust gas to improve the flow of free air. The early turbos were very basic indeed.

Two snail-shaped housings, which, with the aid of a rubber hose, would let air in. The out connection was connected directly to the exhaust with the spinning rotor enclosed.

Neither of these components generally went wrong. The fault generally was in the centre housing.

In the very early days, parts were not available. This was a challenge. I'll show you what we do here. Usually, the preamble for *I have no idea*.

The part was stripped and examined. The fault was obvious, the bearing had overheated. With hindsight, we understand that both great heat and great speed are achieved when it's working.

All other parts appeared to be serviceable, and we assumed these were OK to reuse.

The centre bearing was a bronze-looking item that floated in oil when it was working properly. It had no ball bearings, just this well-made, solid, precision block of bronze.

The size was established exactly. Then it was turned down using our trusty lathe. To bring it back to its original size, solder was used. In fact, more than was necessary.

It then had to be machined to exactly the same diameter as the original bearing. I have to say that we had this off to a fine art. We had repaired more than ten, and they all spun by hand.

The commercial vehicles these were fitted to were basic, it took only twenty minutes to remove the turbo. We had various successes with the early repairs. Most lasted until the engine got hot. One actually lasted a month, only eleven months short of our warranty period.

A halt was called to this repair, only for a short time. The manufacturer had released a repair kit. This included the centre bush, or bearing as it was known.

We had quite a lot of success on the old vehicles, but with more complex adaptions and add-ons, balancing the shafts became an issue. We gave up.

10-7 The Polished Element

In a fuel injection pump, there is a part called an element. It's correct name is Plunger and Barrel.

It's a machined part with two matching pieces. The barrel is a fixed part usually locked in the pump body. The plunger goes up and down at a predetermined amount dictated by a camshaft. The plunger can also rotate, allowing the fuel delivery to vary as it turns.

This is activated by an angled sloped cut within the plunger, located by a hole in the barrel. This is generally the heart of a diesel pump, although things have since moved on. The main issue with any diesel system is poor fuel quality.

These precision parts are lubricated by the diesel fuel itself, so cleanliness is essential. Our helpful bricklayer's bucket is not a very good place to transport diesel.

Likewise, the holding tank without a filler cap also shortens the fuel pump's life. Any contamination adversely affects the pump.

The fuel filter is fitted (or maybe not) to collect solid debris from the system. It takes out sand, gravel, mud, sludge, and even paper, but it isn't good with fluids. Once the filter is full, it cannot cope, and it shuts down or, worse, it lets particles by. In the end, lots of particles. All are abrasive, and wear soon occurs.

It is always good to show a customer a failed component. He may not understand the workings but can see the results of erosion.

Dumpty had it planned to this end. In his pocket was a very, very contaminated element. This was from a pump that was running at a quarry. Sandstone dust was always an issue.

When new, the element is polished. This one had lines the whole way down due to the dust. The scores in the plunger were huge. Getting a fingernail to feel them was like using an emery board. This element was as bad as they get.

On numerous occasions, Dumpty would produce this element from his pocket. Always advising the customer that the cause of his problem was contamination.

"Look," he would say. "This was from your pump. See the big scores in it."

Some three years on, the rusty and worn element had lost most of the rust. Most of it had rubbed off into Dumpty's coat pocket. By now, the element looked as good as new. It gleamed. It still had the scores but was less effective.

What I learned from that element was to show the customers where their money was spent.

It was a good ploy, but actually, only show them the parts that genuinely came from their own pump.

10-8 Wine

A cultured liquid enjoyed by many after a hard day's toil. Normally produced abroad and served in bottles.

Dumpty had a British challenger to the European model. His new hobby was to manufacture a brew he called "Dumpty's Fine Wine". That, it wasn't. It tasted at best of turps or creosote. It was dangerous if swallowed. Undeterred, he was manufacturing it in ever greater quantities.

A flagon was now available for tasting. This was commonplace. To align the subtleness of the brew, clean plastic beakers were also available for tasting. After the first month, over ninety beakers out of the pack of one hundred were still gathering dust.

It was being offered to all, staff, customers, he was even trying to sell it at tea break in the canteen.

The end of this chapter came abruptly.

We were visited by our major franchise holder, and yes, the wine appeared. All wisely declined for two reasons. They had been pre-warned of the quality and danger of the product.

The second excuse was that they had not brought enough toilet rolls with them. One of our directors saw the brew while passing by to meet the guests.

Angrily, he told Dumpty to get it off the site, NOW.

Everybody gave sighs of relief when it was all packed away in Dumpty's car boot. To my knowledge, no customers were lost although he had tried his best. Bless him.

10-9 Oil Heaters

One of good old Dumpty's self-beliefs was in his ability to repair the company's oil heaters. Generally, they did not work if it was cold. Very often, they did not work at all.

He enlisted the trusted Desmo as a brave assistant engineer. Press ganged is more accurate. The professional company used for servicing and maintenance were expensive and unreliable.

Sam 48 (My Way)

The theory was good, we had an abundance of old engine oil. What better way than to make good use of this product—saves money, keeps us warm and is low maintenance.

Save money it did, we froze, as the heaters rarely worked. Maintenance was every hour on the hour, fiddling with the burner or something similar. One particular morning, it was well below the freezing point, and the heater had not come on.

The casing was removed, and a blockage was found just before the pilot glow-light. The blockage was removed, and Dumpty shouted to Desmo, "Push the ignition button."

The order of events that followed was hysterical. At least for anybody watching.

Firstly, oil flowed and sprayed over Dumpty. He jerked back, luckily, and avoided any injury. With Dumpty just a foot away, the oil ignited. There was a sort of bang, and the burner came to life.

Dumpty had caught full-on the carbon black dust and grime that was static on the burner. It resembled ash in the old type of coal fire you cleaned out the next morning.

Dumpty was covered from the waist up. He looked the opposite of a flower grader. Once his glasses were removed, he was recognisable, without the Caribbean look-alike anymore.

A few more instances similar to this, and he conceded that the agents needed reinstating.

10-10 Chads

This character has been around forever, it seems. Dumpty did not like it. Everybody has love-and-hate images, but this was his pet hate.

The image is of an egg-shaped head with its nose hanging over a brick wall. Stevie knew this and could produce this drawing in seconds. Also, on his notepad, about every fifth page had one or more.

I remember the wall calendar for June, having one with a speech bubble, "Remember me from February."

They were everywhere. Cut-out ones even in his jacket pocket.

There was a new pack of paper for the photocopier that appeared sealed. It had been got at. A giant Chad had been drawn on one sheet. It was photocopied probably twenty times.

It must have taken hours to interspace the sheets evenly and repack them into the packaging. Once opened, the paper was, of course, looking like it was new, but here he was again.

This irritant went on for years.

10-11 Threepenny Bit Tyres

Tyres should be round, black and made of rubber. They need balancing to provide smooth driving.

Many years ago, captain Dumpty obtained an engine with some issues. This was going to be transplanted into his own vehicle, which was past its best.

The engine was stripped and checked over by the good man. It was going to be repaired on the cheap.

I suggested the crankshaft was out of specification, thus needing regrinding. This would have a reasonable cost, but it would be a professional repair.

He turned deaf ears to my suggestion. Just a set of new bearings and an oversize thrust to take up the slack, was his opinion.

His money, his choice.

It was rebuilt with the above spares and with an air gun. No, not with a torque wrench, that would take too much time. The engine looked good from the outside, it had been housed in our cleaner for a couple of weeks.

He did buy a new gasket kit, but even that was a suspect cheap and nasty copy. Trying to turn the engine by hand proved difficult. No. Impossible is accurate.

Showing no sign of concern, Dumpty fitted the engine to his Cortina.

When engaged, the starter motor just went "clonk". The engine was rock solid. Not to be beaten by an inert piece of metal, he used the service van for assistance. The tow rope was attached to his chariot and to the hook on the van.

Worzel was towing Dumpty downhill in the yard. As he attempted to bump-start the car, the rope broke. Undeterred, he replaced the rope with a strong chain, and they were off. The route was about three miles around the block.

As Dumpty let the clutch engage, the rear wheels were dragged along the tarmac. The engine was static. The suggestion to go faster before bumping, he thought, may help.

About every hundred yards, there were tyre skid marks where the wheels were locking.

On his return to the workshop, he found that the rear tyres were wrecked. They had flat spots all around. Defeat was never conceded, but the engine was again removed and the crankshaft reground.

It was never a really good engine, even after the better repair, but it did at least turn over and run.

The car received a couple of second-hand replacement tyres. This, along with a new clutch that was destroyed in the attempt to bump the car.

Under my breath, I muttered, "Told you so."

10-12 The Navy Lark

We received a call from the Naval Dockyard in Chatham about a ship that was in trouble. To Dumpty's delight, it was a real ship, we had been called to assist the Navy.

It was an Ice Breaker and was in for a major refit, so Bosch needed a local dealer to assist. We were met by two of the Bosch UK service team at the security gate with documents in order.

Dumpty had been advised not to wear his wartime medals as it could have offended our hosts.

Of course, Bosch is an international brand but was formally a German state company. Gert and Eric from Bosch, along with Dumpty and myself, now had boarding passes.

My immediate concern was to hope they did not want us to attend the main engines. Relief followed as the two donkey engines that ran the generators were passing diesel into the engine oil.

The engineer in charge looked like Captain Birdseye. He was requested to drain both engines and fill them with fresh engine oil.

The Bosch Engineers had brought a flow metre and were busy calculating the viscosity of the oil.

I said to Dumpty if the level was an inch up the dipstick that is a 10 percent dilution. Soon after, the viscosity results were published from the printer with a finding of dilution of 9.4 percent.

Dumpty suggested they change the oil filters also. His bulky size struggled.

The marine engineer grunted because it was a tight fit to the safety rails. Discussions were going on about the cause of dilution when Dumpty came to the fore.

On the side of the generators' main fuel pump was a lift pump that gathered diesel from the tank. This was removed from the side of the pump, and a blanking plate fitted where the lift pump was.

Once the engine was started, a continual drip was seen by all from this lift pump. This task was repeated on the second engine with the same results.

We were comfortable taking the two lift pumps back to the base and fitting two service kits. The following day, Dumpty and I returned to fit the repaired items.

Their engineer wanted to carry out the same test as before. Fortunately, no drips. Now happy, he fitted them both and shook our hands for the success.

10-13 The Navy Lark Continues

Following our success with the oil dilution issues, it was still early doors.

With Dumpty's charm for all things boats, we had the administrator on our side with his tales about the MTB (Motor Torpedo Boats) during the war, dodging the Japanese fleet, yes, he was a hero. We were taken to the feeding station, that is, the land-based civilian mess.

Everything was supplied, care of the Navy, who operated this function. We then had a guided tour of the site, quite an eye-opener. They made rope, proper rope, some over a foot thick. Also, proper flags.

We went to the engineering shop, which had equipment you could only dream of. They had a shear shaft from the boat we were attending, this had sheared.

The shaft joins the engine to the propellor and is a safety device to prevent damage. Should the propellor get tangled with rope, it would stop turning very quickly. The powerful engine still powers the gearbox to the propellor.

The idea of the shaft is to break and disconnect the engine to the propellor instantly. Once the propellor is freed from rope or weed, it is free to rotate again.

A new shaft is fitted and all is well. Off we go again.

The machine shop had manufactured eleven of these shafts. This, before they had one to shear in the same place as the pattern.

It took many memos from the engineer to explain that as long as it sheared, where did not matter. The estimated cost of these shafts was about £2000. Each.

The machine shop had manufactured an initial six shafts, but all sheared, not at the same position as the original. Six more were made, all four feet long, solid, heavy steel roller over eight inches in diameter.

Splines were cut precisely along the whole length so that it would marry to the couplings at either end of the transmission. The centre section was then machined down to about half the diameter of its original size.

Further machining added further reductions, but all six at different lengths from the end.

Shaft number eleven sheared in an identical position as the original. A cheer went up, success was here. Six more shafts were produced. No need to test as the shear point had been established.

These were to be carried by the ship as spares.

10-14 It Goes On

This refit of the Montgomery Ice Breaker was well over budget. It was docked for many a month.

The two gangplanks allowed access while it was docked. The maintenance staff had colour-coded overalls for recognition.

Brown was cleaning staff, Blue was crew, White was senior crew, and it went on. Green were painters, Black were electricians. Orange was the cooking brigade, and others I know not.

There were two characters at the forward gangplank. Their task was to count the number of people entering the ship. For this exercise, the colour of the workwear mattered.

There were a lot of people getting on the ship, and all had been counted. The ship's complement of sailors is about four hundred when in service. Surprisingly, over 11,000 had boarded the vessel in one day.

This number of people would have made the ship severely list if they all stood on one side. Many had done the round trip, on at the front and off at the back. Some entered the ship over thirty times making a mockery of the head count. No one was checking the other gangplank.

Time and motion were not popular with the dock workers. I think the ship never returned to service; it was sold off.

As was the dockyard, many moaned, but then they became unemployed.

Who won? We did. We got paid handsomely and ate a wonderful breakfast.

Chapter 11
Toilets and Cubicles

11-1 The Toilet Block

We, in fact, had two in our workshop area.

The "Ladies" was obviously their palace, so no known issues existed. Although on one occasion we did put a notice on the door. Blocked again, please take care.

But the "Gents" was a different experience and a challenge. Three wall washbasins. A central, round communal basin with a chrome centre pedestal with soap dispensers.

Water was delivered by operating a circular tread-rail by foot, which was also circular to the pedestal. The basin, as it was known, looked like the budget version of the famous Trevi Fountain in Rome.

There existed a wall-mounted urinal and four individual cubicles.

11-2 Georgiou

All the above were kept well in order by Georgiou, a character, one of identical twins who are hard to forget.

A green card gentleman who was employed to clean and maintain the toilet blocks and clean leaves and the rubbish outside.

Georgiou stuttered but was a lovable character who worked for many a year as Sanitary Inspector–Grade 1.

Their cherished Skoda was at least 20 years old but kept on the road by helpful technicians because we could. I think no repair invoices ever surfaced for the Skoda, even for the MOT test.

One of their claims to fame was the M25 ring road—165 miles travelled at 50 mph and three hours for the trip.

They went from Dartford to Dartford but did not know it was that far away. Georgiou did not drive. His brother had the licence. Only once around the M25! Georgiou must have been reading the map.

11-3 The Cubicles

The cubicles had doors with an external pull handle and an internal lock.

There were normally a couple of floor mops on hand to clean any excess water from the floor as daily cleaning was deemed a requirement.

The same mop could also be placed through the pull handle and across the door frame. Exit from the cubicle was then not possible other than by climbing over a high door.

Enter Jack, a creature of habit, who punctually and regularly attended this area. One could say you could set your watch by this repetition.

Jack was a Northern chap, very strong, heavy but slow in movement and had a heavy, chesty cough.

The hand rags we used for everyday cleaning were stored in a sack ready for contract cleaning. When welding, there was always a danger that one could catch fire.

They did not catch alight, but it was more like they smouldered, which was almost impossible to put out. Two or three were lit up and slid under the door, and a wheel trolley was propped against the door to keep them inside.

Looking from a safe distance, smoke was seen billowing from the open windows of trap three. We removed all obstacles from the door and ran like hell. Oaths were issued in our absence.

11-4 The Fountain

The chrome centre piece was robust, it needed to be. On occasion, victims were bound and placed in this contraption.

With hands and feet cable-tied together and an additional cable tied around the fountain's turret, the victim was captured. He was unable to move and needed a final rinse for hygiene purposes.

Soap was applied liberally, not to cleanse the victim but to make the contact surface of the porcelain more slippery.

The victim could be spun, I think about five revolutions is one of the best spins recorded.

Nobody was brave enough to remain present, so any local, heavy object could be positioned on the tread rail. Warm water would flow continually until the foot rail is released.

Approximately 20 minutes were needed to wash the subject. including all the undergarments. Soap and water went everywhere, except the volume the apprentice retained in his workwear. On one occasion, Meat Ball, the truck service manager walked into the washroom. Seeing that the fountain was in full use, he just used the hand basin, dried his hands and left.

Not a word to the soggy apprentice, whose hopes for an assisted quick release were dashed.

11-5 The Stretcher

Being safety conscious, a stretcher was attached to a wall bracket and kept folded for use, if required.

Never seen in action until Lummi slipped on some soap in the washroom.

Two of us were dispatched to get the stretcher as a first-aider attended to the wounded Lummi. We placed the stretcher flat on the floor next to Lummi and unfolded the contraption quickly.

A mixture of brake dust, iron fillings, crisp packets and other garage waste was piled onto Lummi.

By now he had regained consciousness but refused to mount the stretcher. A small dust cloud formed, and any litter present was waved away.

Lummy was pronounced alive at the scene.

We suspected a bruised forehead was better than a crisp-wrapped case of asbestosis. The stretcher was refolded and positioned suitably to gain the maximum amount of garbage.

11-6 First-Aid Box

The first-aid box was about as good as the stretcher.

It should have been serviced and replenished each quarter by contractors.

The contents had been removed or maybe even used except for one small plaster. Inside were two of Barnes' late cards from the tech college and a safety pin.

The prize of the box was a plastic frog, which had a battery inside. It had been there for some time. The battery was flat.

11-7 The Deflector

Some members of the workforce were a little shy and preferred to use the cubicles rather than the urinals.

We assisted with their preference by placing a layer of clingfilm under the seat cover. This was reserved for Saturdays only. Why? I don't know.

No major issues but very off-putting when urgent relief was necessary.

More of an irritant than a genuine prank, but it still was a must-do job on the list.

Chapter 12
The New Building

12-1 The Search

I had the good fortune (or not) to be promoted to Departmental Manager with a promise of new premises soon.

At heart, I was still Sam. I was the mature apprentice, now in charge of all that was diesel. I, along with my Assistant Manager, went and looked at many properties that showed great potential.

All had issues, too big, too small, too expensive, next to a nun's house, might flood, a lion once lived next door and so on.

12-2 Next Door

A master stroke by the company was the purchase of a garage that was next door to ours. It was now made for a very large area between the railway line and the main A20.

This acquisition was split into three sections, and we were given the old centre section. This old building was a nightclub just before the war, in fact, the upstairs flooring was still the original.

A sound structure but mature with much to be done, moving equipment and stock, fitting out the unit and much more. The old corrugated asbestos roof had a hole about the size of a two-pound coin.

I got estimates for repairing the roof and one for replacing the whole asbestos roof.

Yuk!

Out of question, was the immediate response for the whole roof replacement. Not in the budget, I was told.

I had the perfect fix.

While moving everything from our old, cramped unit, anything that had no home was put upstairs. From our reception, there was a tired, wilting cheese plant in a giant pot. This had been lacking love.

I dragged this potted triffid some thirty feet and placed it directly under the hole in the roof. Everyone had smiles on their faces and a shekel was saved.

The MD said jokingly, "Now, you are thinking like an experienced manager."

Thinking without speaking, I thought saved thousands. Perhaps a raise of a penny an hour. No chance!

Loving care (watering) added to the triffid's life and now, a permanent roof repair.

12-3 My Former Boss

He was a gentleman. I had and still have the utmost respect for him.

As I explained, at the beginning of my time with the company, it was he who had employed me. I think he had sound judgement with the staff taken on, with foresight into development and expansion.

I, and over two hundred staff, all depended on his capacity to make sound decisions. Company loyalty was evident although the pay was generally lean.

His loyalty to staff was shown annually by an event Mr D cherished for many a year. The function in question was dinner at one of the best local hotels. All expenses paid.

Everybody who had worked for a period of twenty-five years or more was invited. At the peak, there were over fifty attendees, some had left but returned, the grass was not greener on the other side.

Split service counted, all having served a minimum of twenty-five years in total were present. This also showed loyalty to the company by these employees, by these excellent numbers.

Over a quarter of the workforce was present, so this left a hole back at the base. Some took it for granted, others were pleased. Some had never eaten in a restaurant before.

Some of the senior management just took it as part of the job but still enjoyed the day. But thank you, Mr D.

Over the years, we noted some of his quirky habits. I will attempt to list a couple. I am sure there were many more.

Lunchtime was usually a McDonalds, one of the usual gofers was dispatched at exactly 1.15pm to collect this.

The order had been phoned through by his trusty secretary who knew his needs before he did.

The gofer quickly returned with this gastronomic delight still hot and knowing that it would fend off his hunger pains.

At 3.15, the same gofer was ready for the National West Bank. The governor and Harry set off. This happened every Friday just as they were closing.

I knew a cashier at this bank, and she said that he always asked for new notes. Always just as they were cashing up for the day.

His secretary, Laura, could tell many a tale but never did.

12-4 The C5 and the Jaguar

One other story of the MD I recall is of the Sinclair C5. This was an accident waiting to happen. This was a predecessor to the electric bicycle that now haunts pavements all over the country.

A journey on the C5 was to go to the new depot some five miles away from the base. Mounting this beast, off he went in a suit and polished shoes, slap bang in the centre of the single-lane road.

Yes, there was now a good traffic jam behind him. The C5 was going slower and slower. Then it stopped, the battery had given its all, and it was only halfway to the destination.

In those days, mobile phones did not exist. The cursed C5 was pushed onto a grass verge.

He did not have to wait too long before somebody from the company was flagged down. By then, he was soaked to the skin. The C5 was mothballed from that day.

Another story was about the first time I saw his anger.

It was shortly after the beginning of my employment. A very dirty and generally knackered old Ford van entered our garage at great speed.

It screeched to a halt by our foreman's office. The MD jumped out in a red rage. His very elegant wife exited the passenger side of the van, looking like the gorgeous model that she was.

The whole workshop could not fail to see her and to hear the commotion. All else was quiet.

His description of the E-Type Jaguar that was his pride and joy, and how it had broken down on the old A20 was worth listening to. He managed to get to a local garage and bought this treasure he had just arrived in for a few quid.

People were dispatched to recover the Jaguar immediately. The van the MD and his wife had arrived in had previously been used for carrying cattle feed and scrap metal. Before he had calmed down, his wife had been escorted to the boardroom, I believe, by a senior accounts woman to get cleaned up.

Her beautiful dress was not looking so good with the rusty marks from an old exhaust pipe added. This was not going to be a day to cross his path.

His passing many years later was a shock to all. He had been unwell for a short period of time, and the buzzword was that he was in the hospital.

I thought we could return some of his kindness, so we obtained a "Get well soon" card. This was hurriedly sent around the company, even reaching all the seven depots within two days.

It was signed by most of the people in the 25-year club and forwarded to Mr D's family to pass on to him.

He did not survive much longer, but I hope it gave him some comfort in his last days.

That was the end of an era.

12-5 Jock

This character hated just about everything. He was a pal of a couple whom he went to day release with.

They told him what a wonderful place they worked at. This ate away at him. He did not like the BMC dealership or the people there.

In no time at all, he joined our company, and yes, we had the moaner. He was given an initial job in the service bay. He was told he would be moved when a vacancy became available. It never did, thank goodness.

He was working next to Deaf Runner Bean on the left lift. On the other side was Larry who had headphones and music on.

He was not happy here either, he had only been with us for just under a year. He was a member of the same working men's club that many of us frequented.

Twenty years on and still complaining, he was to be avoided if you could. His best mate was an odd fellow called Blinkey. He was almost an albino and spent a lot of time in Thailand. Jock had now completed his 25 years of service.

The Friday presentation had gone off well, he had been quiet throughout.

Sam 48 (My Way)

We converged at our club for the usual Friday night pint, when Jock started up. "I have worked for 25 years at this rundown dump, and all they give you is a mangy watch. I would have preferred some cash instead," he moaned.

A full one hundred pounds bought Jock's watch. It was engraved with his name and the year. These watches were from Garretts of London and cost our company hundreds of pounds. Soon after Jock left our company, he moved with Blinkey to Thailand.

I never saw Jock again, but he did receive a very small company pension.

The word was that with his huge comparable wealth, he was the Mayor of the village. He and Blinkey married a couple of young, beautiful ladies, we heard.

I just wonder if he still moans or just groans.

Chapter 13
Our Claim to Fame

13-1 The Bucking Bronco

A very narrow Ford tractor was introduced to the already popular and expanding Ford range. This slim tractor was aimed at the vineyard market, which at that time had no direct competitor.

Our company sold its fair share, one customer bought 16, all in a single order. All was well for a couple of months. Then the tractor was reported to be bucking.

This meant that without touching the throttle, the tractor lurched forward out of the driver's control.

The driver's report was that he stopped at vine one, attempted to slowly move to vine two, but ended up at vine four.

Clearly, there was an issue. All of Mr Bartholomew's tractors were developing the same issues.

I suggested they plant the vines further apart but was immediately told I was out of order. Two tractors were brought to our base workshop.

After onboard checks of the tractor were carried out, the fault was confirmed to be within the fuel pump.

The first pump was removed and sent to us as a warranty repair. We stripped the pump, changed all the necessary standard parts and found no fault at all. We bench-tested the pump and gave it a clean bill of health.

The Tractor Sales Manager phoned us because once the pump was refitted to the engine, it was worse than ever. The second repair to the second tractor was only marginally better.

Ford was contacted, and they acknowledged that there may be an issue.

My foreman was a master technician and had completed all the training courses with distinction. After a discussion, he and an apprentice went to our tractor depot on the other side of town. We had specialist equipment that the average tractor mechanic could only dream of.

Different fuel was used, oil added to the diesel, the engine timing checked and many other tests carried out. It was established that the pump pressure was building up and releasing quickly.

Just as the fuel release occurred, off went the tractor in a hop with its two front wheels off the ground.

Two days in, and the pump was off the vehicle again. Lengthy telephone calls with the manufacturers took place. Discussions trying to pinpoint the gremlin were ongoing, clearly unofficial as the manufacturer would not commit.

My foreman suspected that a shaft within the pump was the root cause of the issue. We discussed the options.

An earlier shaft from a different model was purchased and fitted within the pump. Within three weeks all 16 of Mr Bartholomew's herd of Broncos were serviced.

We vowed not to tell the trade the fix. Soon pumps were arriving from near and far. At one time, we had three technicians building and testing these.

The Ford team came down for a visit to try and find our magic fix. They were none the wiser.

Some 8000 of these tractors had now been sold in the UK, and the fault was well-known. The warranty was paying us handsomely for fixing the issue with these pumps, and our fame spread far and wide.

We had repaired about 15 percent of the total in the UK with great success, but the end was nigh.

I was asked to attend a meeting in our boardroom by my MD the following day. After a sleepless night, my MD and four German People from the German head factory were present.

Two spoke perfect English, and I was interrogated about our success. The heavy German was from research and development. He had not spoken.

He had all our warranty claims on his laptop. I was asked why the parts listed were fitted. It was now getting tricky.

We claimed to have fitted new shafts, part number 314 as per the parts list.

The heavy German was checking our purchases. We had only bought three of that numbers in five years. "EUREKA!" he cried. He had found our purchase record for shaft 311, which was our fix.

We had purchased over 1000 in the last three years. I explained we had to put the correct build part number on the claim to get the claim accepted.

The Germans all went home, mission accomplished. After their investigation, a service bulletin came through with the modification of part numbers.

Congratulations were handed to my foreman and me for earning the company so much money. Each fix paid our company just shy of £500. For each repair.

Just imagine the many problems all across Europe that are now resolved.

13-2 Smoking Area

During our move to our luxury apartments, the smoking rules changed.

We had three smokers in our section who now had good cause to have a cigarette every hour.

Hand washing, journey to the designated area, puffing the fag, returning to the workstation, 15 minutes lost every hour.

I just could not resist the opportunity to add my touch to this unfair situation. One area excelled on every count. It had a low bench, which was uncomfortable, eight feet square with a 4 x 4 wooden frame. Portable was an understatement.

Perspex corrugated sheets were lashed onto three sides of the frame, making this a legal structure. Time limits were introduced, and the nearby steps also had a health and safety camera fixed to view the shed.

I waited until the working day had finished. My timing was right.

Firstly, putting a cardboard box over the camera, the unknown practical joker struck. The wooden frame of this new smoking shed now had four NO SMOKING signs firmly attached. Glued and nailed.

This did not totally fix the problem, but it sure brought the shed to the attention of the directors. Our workshop was far better and safer with smoking banned.

The non-smokers were grateful for the steps taken to comply with the current changes.

Chapter 14
Tools and Cash

14-1 New Specialist Tools

When a new model of a vehicle is produced, all the main dealers have specialist tools delivered as part of the franchise deal.

The new model in question had tools with the value of about £4000. The usual carriers had a good rapport with us and offloaded three very heavy boxes, which I signed for.

Recognising the sender's name as the tool manufacturer, I assumed the contents were for car service. I phoned the Car Service Manager. Let's call him Kevin The Creep.

He moaned and sent a man with a boy to collect the tools in their own service van.

Got rid of that, I thought, as the three huge boxes were very heavy and clogged our reception.

Some three months went by, and one of our company directors phoned me. The tools were missing, and my signature was on the manifest. It was made clear that it was my neck on the block.

I thought that was a bit fierce, but I needed to be calm, and a cunning plan was needed. I asked for 24 hours to see if I could assist with the problem.

I was the chief subject in the tool's disappearance. My card was marked, so I had to try to prove that I had no knowledge of the theft. I obtained a copy of the receipt with my signature, yes, it was mine.

Sam 48 (My Way)

It included the three parcel numbers. Ken, the chap who collected the tools with the van, had since retired. He had the memory of an amoeba when I phoned him at his home. So, no help there.

Spyglass in hand, my detective instincts came to the fore. I had the package numbers. With a copy of the numbers from this manifest, I needed to try to find the boxes and labels.

Three boxes of tools weighing about a hundred pounds each. Where could they be!

I could not recall selling them for scrap. I would not be that stupid. I went to the car service foreman, Town.

He gave me the key to the tool store as I needed to borrow a fictitious spacer for our press. Once in the tool store, within minutes, I found the three boxes unopened. Now, for some sport, me thinks.

I cut the three labels from the boxes. I did not open them, and I planned my next move. I gave Town the spacer back, which we didn't really need, along with the tool store key.

Sport, it was to be. I phoned the director and told him the good news. He appeared happy at first.

Welcoming me into his office, he said, "What news of this disaster?"

My answer was that I had managed to track down the boxes I had signed for.

He then said, "How do I know these are the same boxes?"

I then produced the three labels from my pocket, which matched the numbers on the manifest sheet.

I laid out the signed sheet and the three labels I had cut from the boxes. My comment then was that I signed for these unopened and, therefore, had no knowledge of the contents.

He then said, "So where were the labels?"

Not letting this go easily, I said, "On the boxes."

Going slightly red and getting slightly angry, I was asked where the tools were.

"I don't know for sure, but I expect they are still in their boxes," I said.

They were the ones with the labels on them that I had signed for. My fun was up. I had made my point.

I said, "Generally, we would expect to find tools in the tool store. That is where I found all three boxes, unopened, with the labels attached."

The amoeba had done well. He had put them exactly where they should have been. My sarcastic comment needed saying!

It was just a pity that the service manager in question didn't know where he had kept his tool. I suggested he keep it in his drawers. I was thanked for my help in solving this tricky situation, and the director welcomed its conclusion.

Kevin The Creep must have had his arse kicked. It all felt worthwhile. Happy Ending!

14-2 Old Unit Box

The parts department was a secure place that held many thousands of pounds of spares. The vehicle manufacturers had an exchange scheme running, which was handy.

Once a customer purchased an exchange part, he needed to return the replaced unit. This ensured that they got the deposit back, making the exchange price cheaper than for new starters, alternators, and anything diesel, which were our targets.

We would raid this box regularly. As long as the headcount was correct, it was OK.

If we had a starter that was totally burnt out, we would switch it with another in this box. Very often, we would only put the obvious visual parts together in a unit.

Sometimes, their weight gave them away. Almost hollow, but all right for the head count. What this was doing, was improving the parts necessary to repair a starter.

The starter sometimes only needed minor parts, costing a few pounds. The absolute meltdown unit was returned for someone else to cherish.

It is fair to say that this saved our company thousands but was unauthorised. We knew all the large companies who were remanufacturing the diesel components under contract to Fords.

Many of the employed technicians meet up on training courses. The chatter is who does what and who for.

Certain fuel pumps were remanufactured by one of my foreman's buddies' companies. We had a very poor pump in, probably terminal, but were saved by the box.

Capturing this prize asset, we managed to make a good profit from this sale. The returned unit was built but hollow. It had a note inside, "Love You."

It was almost two years later that my foreman got a phone call from his mate Ian. He thanked him for his love letter. We admitted nothing, but a lot of humour flowed. The good old days.

14-3 The Cash Box

Each month, Mindy used to travel throughout the company and check the float money in the petty cash boxes.

We had a nominal twenty-five quid float. Each month, this was a challenge. I used to bank in town and would collect five pounds worth of pennies. Another five pounds in five and ten pence pieces. These were fair exchange for a 10-pound note. Therefore, the cash box was always heavy.

Mixed in with this abundance of change, were some worthless Tunisian Dinars. There were some out-of-date Turkish coins just in case an old Turk should arrive.

Mindy stacked the coins in piles while counting them, a quick jolt, and down they went. The float was present, Mindy gave me a receipt and took away the small change.

The following day, fifteen pounds were returned to the tin in note form.

After the weekend, the small change reappeared. I had swapped it back for the notes. The Dinar, Drachma, Rouble and Paise we had collected added to the confusion.

We were proud to announce the two hours spent on petty cash checks were worthwhile. Over an hour was needed to balance ours.

Chapter 15

The New PC System

15-1 All Hail the System

As a medium-sized company, a good computer system is essential for us.

Our new chief of operations was the guy charged with organising the most suitable system to be purchased.

High Pants, as he was known, was brilliant academically but lacked nous. Me, being old school and computer dim, saw a challenge looming.

I booked a course at the local PC training centre and grasped the basics. I was sent by the company to the UK training centre for the PC system that had been purchased.

It was as beneficial as a submarine sitting on a beach in the sun. The benefits were that I stayed at a Toby Inn, so I was well-fed.

I did pass the course, however, as Susie, one of our receptionists, filled out the exam answer sheet for me. She had worked on this type of system for years at her previous employment.

15-2 The Impossible Task

After being told, "You will change to the new system and not it, to your old ways," the challenge was on.

First line—Vehicle Registration.

Second line—Mileage.

Both were essential for producing an invoice, without which you cannot proceed. Now, in comes farmer Giles with a set of injectors out of his 30-year-old digger.

It has no registration plate, no mileage. Mr Giles does not know how to put oil in it let alone who made it.

I put the question to High Pants.

He grunted and said, "Make up some details," to overcome this glitch.

Sport was on again. Micky Mouse 1—the first invoice was produced. So on and so forth. My instruction was clear. Make up some details.

Many Micky Mouse invoices now existed with, of course, hard paper copies that were correct. We now had a file, alphabetically holding these invoices.

We had purchased a small safe to keep the cash that was mounting up. Naturally, everything was building up.

By the month-end, we had to separate the cash sales from the account sales. With internal sales, there was no VAT charged, so a third holding group became necessary.

15-3 Sales Dip

There was a sudden drop in sales, turnover was down, all very evident.

A meeting was called. High Pants sat opposite me. The directors and many accounts staff were all present.

I showed the two hundred and sixty-seven invoices in the incomplete, pending section. The total value was a small fortune.

I explained that we were not consulted before the system was installed but were insulted when it was installed. "It did not work for us," was my answer.

High Pants called it just a glitch.

The MD was not so understanding. "Why was this problem not foreseen?" he asked.

Sam 48 (My Way)

I had enough of the big brother culture growing daily, it was ever-present and gaining momentum. It was just at that moment in time that I felt the light had just come on.

I knew it was about time for me to part company and seek a fresh challenge. "They forgot the 6 Ps," I commented.

There was quite a pause and then silence.

"Perfect Planning Prevents Piss Poor Performance." I explained, "These are the 6 Ps."

If looks could kill, I would have been dead. The silence seemed to last forever.

After this meeting, my time with the company was limited, but I had suffered enough anyway.

I was thanked for my input, and the meeting continued without me.

I was told later that serious failures were unfolding. This was just one example. We were given a code instead of a registration number. This started at 11, our department's code. Funny registrations, but consecutive—11 GB 00001.

The mileage also now worked. This time, enter just 00001 and off we went. About forty-plus invoices for cash sales were knocked off daily. The first dozen invoices generated over six grand, paid in from our cash box.

The following day, a further large amount of cash was paid in, and, yes, it all balanced.

On the third day, the cash box was empty, fortunately, along with every cash sales invoice. We then paid catch-up with the account sales.

Various customers had, with our aid, overloaded their budget limit. It was always overridden, so just the internal sales to go.

Within that month, we cleared the entire backlog, along with the jobs in hand. Our monthly meeting to update the board was larger than usual. There were board members present, thanking us for catching up.

Averaging the three months' sales, the figures were acceptable but not brilliant. I said they were never going to be with the system that was introduced. It was too slow and inaccurate.

A point that was proven to all present when my copy of the accounts had half the internal sales that theirs had.

Not helped and stated from a solid base, I said, "The accounts staff couldn't count."

When checked, it was found that many retail sales with VAT were included. Just another mapping issue. I was thanked for my input, and I left before arses were kicked.

15-4 Time to Go

Eventually, I did master the PC system, but it was so time-consuming and user-unfriendly, it was almost a joke. Capped off by the very helpful Mark Arse, the IT guru who knew all and even more, he thinks.

Praise be to Mark Arse!

"If the PC system is down, do not phone. Email me," was his answer.

As there had been no movement on my PC, by 11.30, he sussed that something was wrong. Marching into my office, he asked sarcastically if we were going to do any work today.

I showed him the email on the screen still saying, "Help - System stuffed yet again," entered at 8.15.

PC not working, email waiting to be sent. What a tart!

Thank goodness for the pen and notepad. We had been working as normal. No. Better than normal. More productive than ever as there was no red tape to hinder us.

I was asked to account for my actions by the general manager. He said having twelve technicians idle for over three and a half hours was not acceptable. We had been reported. My notepad rescued me.

We had improved efficiency, selling more hours than we worked. This was until the PC system came back online.

Chapter 16
Some of the Staff and Supporting Cast

Split Pin: Major in the fireside lancers, scrooge, grumpy money manager

Mrs What: A gem, really managed the money

Laura Grow: Secretary to the MD, smart, sharp, comical and discreet, good girl

Brenda: Three Thursdays

Joe See: Sugar Plumb fairy, heart of gold, lonely, honest, went too soon

Santander: The road runner, Captain Chaos, honest and loyal

High Pants: Tart

The Late Tricey: Ran the Social Club and more, taken too soon

The Late Ronaldo: Jake The Peg, also taken too soon

Smiffy: Had it away

Tres: Blagged it all the way

Blackie: Aloof and overcooked, assistant tart

Taffy: Best bacon rolls ever

Jacko: The Dart and Odd Job

Jane W: Entertaining

Chas: Left-wing locksmith, a very good man

Di: Elegant and professional but wasted

Jule: The cat lady, wasted

Sara: Sat on her legs
Small Sid: Needed a box
DTM: Sales manager, Dead to Miserable
Parts Sid: Only kept three pistons, why?
Mumbo: School friend and character
Nassar: Not to be upset, football—his life
Bronco: Guitarist and good footballer
Meat Ball: Loved the Library
Minkie: Liked a weight
Gladdole The Elder: Got it right
Gladdole The Younger: Showed him the way
Dino: One hombre
Vic No Toes: Unbalanced
Pete Juggler: Respected Service Manager
Robbie Juggler: Half the man
Brockie: Enjoyed secretarial services
Kathy: Knew far too much
Toppo: Got out
Paddy: The bike
Shep: Unique, master technician
Rose: Worked well and always underpaid
Gladys (Gurt): Very old-fashioned professional
Brownie: Engineering on the kitchen table
Barnie: Cricket scores on fag packet
Harpic: Got around everybody's bend
Knotty: Nutty
Bob W: Never appreciated
Bob L: Never his fault
Brov: Liked his beer

Hud: Impersonated the MD perfectly
May The T: Colourblind sparkie
May The R: My chauffeur
Wiggie Watson: Never caught
Sid Hickie: All coins in the wage packet he kept
Scary Mary: Pussycat
Tom Oldman: Could only drive in first gear

Many others qualify but I'm unable to list all who helped shape my life. People you meet have a great influence on what you are.

Balancing the input from some and ignoring the others is the key. In life, their actions can reflect on who you become.

I thank my family and friends for their support in my life of chaos and enjoyment. A special mention of thanks to the late Mr D who employed me.

Notwithstanding all the above happenings, I believe the investment in me paid off. Some events have been omitted as police prosecution could still be an issue.

Forty-seven years of undetected crime, adventure, misbehaviour and a generally good time.

Then another door opened just before the parting of our ways. It was by far the best result that I could ever have imagined. Maybe I should have done it sooner.

All characters are fictional (or maybe not?) All the above is fictional (or is it?)

D C SAM
Love U All

www.ingramcontent.com/pod-product-compliance
Lightning Source LLC
Chambersburg PA
CBHW071203070526
44584CB00019B/2902